The
Future
European
Model

THE FUTURE EUROPEAN MODEL

Economic Internationalization and Cultural Decentralization

J. ØRSTRØM MØLLER

Foreword by James A. Baker III

Praeger Studies on the 21st Century

 PRAEGER

Westport, Connecticut

Library of Congress Cataloging-in-Publication Data

Møller, J. Ørstrøm.
    The future European model : economic internationalization and
cultural decentralization / J. Ørstrøm Møller / foreword by James A. Baker III.
       p.   cm.—(Praeger studies on the 21st century. ISSN 1070–1850)
    Includes bibliographical references and index.
    ISBN 0–275–95012–3 (alk. paper).—ISBN 0–275–95187–1 (pbk.)
    1. Europe—Economic integration.   2. European Union countries.
I. Title.
HC241.M626   1995
337.1'4—dc20   94–21688

British Library Cataloguing in Publication Data is available

Copyright © 1995 by J. Ørstrom Møller

Library of Congress Catalog Card Number: 94–21688
ISBN: 0–275–95012–3
    0–275–95187–1 (pbk.)
ISSN: 1070–1850

First published in 1995

Praeger Publishers, 88 Post Road West, Westport, Connecticut 06881
An imprint of Greenwood Publishing Group, Inc.

Printed in the United States of America

The paper used in this book complies with the
Permanent Paper Standard issued by the National
Information Standards Organization (Z39.48–1984).

10 9 8 7 6 5 4 3 2 1

Contents

Foreword

When interested observers comment on the future direction of Europe, they often focus on issues such as economics and monetary affairs, foreign and security policies, and enlargement. These are, no doubt, important matters. But looking back over the course of the last half century of European history, the factor I find most striking is the role of certain individuals in generating a lively competition of ideas about the Europe of tomorrow. After all, it is the people of Europe, embracing such ideas, who have over the course of a relatively short time in history created a vital new model of continental relations out of the rubble of a Europe long at war with itself.

It is the task, indeed the duty, of each new generation of Europeans to continue this debate, this search for a unified and prosperous Europe, at peace with itself and a constructive contributor to global progress. Particularly now, as Europe struggles with the end of the Cold War, the completion of the Single Market, and the aftermath of the Maastricht Treaty, there is a need for thoughtful Europeans to look freshly at new conditions so as to frame a new vision of the future. As European officials and their publics begin to consider the items likely to be on the agenda of the 1996 intergovernmental Conference, they would be well-advised to consider the strategic context of this era.

Ørstrøm Møller's book, *The Future European Model,* is in the tradition of those important European individuals who have ventured to lead the way for their compatriots. As a Dane, Mr. Møller prizes an independent outlook; as a European, he is committed to an evolving European integration that suits new conditions in the economy, society, technology, politics, and culture. The heart of Mr. Møller's thesis is the reconciliation of what might appear to some as contradictory trends, economic internationalization, and cultural decentralization.

I explored a similar idea in a speech I gave to the Aspen Institute, Berlin in 1991 on "The Euro-Atlantic Architecture," a companion statement to another policy speech I gave in Berlin in 1989. As the Cold War was winding down, I thought it was important to try to identify those elements of change that we needed to address through post-Cold War structures. One European phenomenon I addressed was the combined and simultaneous devolution and evolution of the nation-state; while I observed some national functions had been delegated "upward" to the then-European Community and Atlantic Alliance in order to deal with challenges of interdependence, other functions had been delegated "downward" to state and local governments, regions, and the private sector, so as to bring government closer to people. In Western Europe, I saw these trends as complementary, indeed interdependent developments, creating a healthy equilibrium. But I warned that the lands to the east faced only the prospect of fragmenting devolution unless balanced by our extension of the structures of trans-Atlantic and European cooperation to them.

I also ventured one other idea that I hope the readers of Mr. Møller's book will consider. To promote cohesion amidst cultural diversity, we still will need a shared commitment to certain ideas. As suggested in 1991, "Throughout the Euro-Atlantic community, and indeed elsewhere around the globe, a fundamental challenge for democracy is to encompass, to represent, but also to transcend ethnic ties on the basis of the common, indeed universal, values." This belief is at the heart of America's concept of nationality. We are a people from many lands bound together by our commitment to certain ideas, not by ties of blood, birth, or creed. These ideas, drawn from the Enlightenment in Europe, are yours as well.

Therefore, as Europeans consider their future structures, as you read Mr. Møller's book, I urge you not to limit your thinking within the borders of geographic propinquity. If Europeans and Americans are to strive for unity of purpose in this new era, our partnership must ultimately draw its strength from a community of values.

James A. Baker III

Preface

In the 1990s we leave behind us the industrial culture and the industrial technology which has three fundamental and far-reaching consequences:

- The political geography imposed by the industrial age comes under strain. The construction of the European Union, the creation of NAFTA and ASEAN, the dissolution of the Soviet Union are all cases in point.
- There will be a shift in weighting among the three vectors of power: military power, economic-financial and technological power, and the power of persuasion—culture, information, and knowledge.
- There will be new players in the international power game: transnational centers and supranational enterprises.

The aim of this book is to trace these new developments, analyze their impact, and draw some conclusions for the prospect of European integration. The basic message is positive. There is evidence to sustain a buoyant view with regard to the future of European integration. What puzzles many European and even more observers from outside Europe is the different role of national state and nationalities in Europe during the next decades. In fact, some of the misunderstandings about European integration can probably be found because of the mix-up of these two notions. Europe stands to benefit from the transition from the industrial age to the immaterial age; however, this change will not take place without substantial social engineering and changes in the political and economic geography. The book points to some of these changes.

ACKNOWLEDGMENTS

I am grateful to Dr. John D. Rockfellow of the Danish Institute for Future Studies without whom this book probably would never have been published. Grethe Kyhl provided help all the way and assistance in typing many versions of the text. Friends and colleagues participated in the discussions that gave rise to many of the ideas put forward in this book. I do not claim "intellectual property rights" of the ideas put forward, but I do assume full responsibility for the text. The text reflects my personal view and is not necessarily congruous with the positions taken by the institutions with which I am or have been connected.

J. Ørstrøm Møller

Organizing European Cooperation

History shows that every European generation makes its own economic and political geography. Many historians take the view that modern political Europe was born in 1648 with the Westphalian peace conference. That can, of course, be disputed, but few would question that the Vienna Congress held in 1815 was the first in a long string of summits that organized the political and economic framework of Europe. On the basis of the Vienna Congress, we can draw a number of lessons to be incorporated into a viable European organization:

- A political and economic geography can withstand the onslaught of time only if it reflects the basic interests of all participants. The treaties do not, in themselves, constitute a power structure. They express the power structure produced by political, cultural, military, and economic interests.
- All actors must take part in the negotiations. If one or several main actors are set aside, they will eventually feel themselves justified in rejecting the result.
- All main actors should approve the result more or less joyfully but certainly not resentfully. They do not need to hail the result, but the achievement is more lasting if that is the case. Probably the best thing is an economic and political geography that is acceptable to everybody with no clear winner or loser.

- The interests of the different nationalities, peoples, and ethnic minorities must be taken into account. Political borders must not violate economic ties, trade links, or religious or cultural traditions. If that happens, a built-in mechanism will trigger conflict or confrontation leading to its breakdown. The Versailles Conference in 1919 and the construction of the Soviet and Russian empires represent the grossest neglect of this principle.
- A political and economic geography is viable only if it can assimilate future developments. This is a tall order because very few people are capable of making reliable forecasts, especially when dealing with such malleable things as the relations among nations, economic interests, technological developments, and cultural patterns.

However, it has been achieved. The Vienna Congress in 1815 understood that after twenty-five years of disturbance, Europe wanted peace above everything else. Even mediocrity met the expectations of Europeans. The founding fathers of European integration in 1949 and 1950 understood, even if they may not have realized it, that Europe needed a framework suitable to further the coming internationalization and multinationalism.

If we were to enlarge the general lessons learned from the Vienna Congress and use not only this agreement but also recent history as a basis for our generalizations, we should add the following theory of democratic inevitability:

> Any regime based on dictatorship and repression must control political information to survive. If this control breaks down so does the state. As soon as nonofficial information starts to spread in the society, either as a result of soldiers bringing news back from the front or through electronic media, the oppressive power structures disintegrate from within. Thus, the development of still more sophisticated means of uncontrolled transnational communication makes it impossible for despots to establish and preserve dictatorship or oligarchy for long periods. The peaceful revolutions of the Central and Eastern European communist regimes, which were steadily spreading from one country to another, are the best examples of this process. Use of the telefax machine during the student revolt in China shows the dominant role of information in the political process. As a result of this, we will witness a chain reaction of current dictatorships being crushed—some slowly and painfully, some swiftly and peacefully.

The construction made at the Vienna Congress lasted about a generation; it broke down in 1848 under the pressure of revolution and nationalism.

After an interim period, the next successful attempt was made in the 1870s. It took place in 1871 with the proclamation of the German empire in Versailles. In 1878 Bismarck took control over the European development at the Berlin Conference. This decade shows Bismarck leading a new German empire to the pinnacle of the European power game. By acts of statesmanship, financial backing, diplomatic skill, political consultations, economic influence, and military clout, the German empire under Bismarck's leadership shaped the European framework. It lasted until 1914. The keyword in Bismarck's diplomacy was restraint exercised by persuasion and skillful maneuvers using military force only when necessary and unavoidable to achieve a well-defined objective.

After World War I, a very fragile European construction was established. Because it did not respect the lessons enumerated above, in less than twenty years it was swept aside by strong underlying forces. After World War II, Europe was organized contrary to much conventional wisdom not at the Yalta and Potsdam conferences in 1945. Shaped, designed, and implemented in 1949–1950 with NATO, OEEC, and the European Coal and Steel Community, it was built upon two strong pillars:

1. A power balance between two blocks. Europe was dichotomized economically, commercially, and culturally. The power balance was ideological and military. A non-European nation (the United States) was brought in to secure equilibrium.

2. The introduction of supranationality. The idea was to incorporate the Federal Republic of Germany in the European construction. This could not be done by the control of Germany by another power. France had tried that in the 1920s with disastrous results. The idea was therefore to amalgamate the industries of six nations in an integrated, institutional framework so that all of them transferred sovereignty to a supranational body in the same sectors, to the same degree and according to the same rules.

Because they were the strategic industries in postwar Europe coal and steel were chosen. Coal and steel controlled the economic development in postwar Europe. Economic reconstruction could take place only if coal and steel were available. The industries also represented a key factor in regard to military rearmament. If the national states did not possess full control over coal and steel they could not rearm. By transferring the management of coal and steel resources from the national to the European level the Europeans carefully husbanded scarce resources while at the same time making individual rearmament impossible.

For the Germans, the French initiative was an offer beyond imagination; one needs only to read Konrad Adenauer's memoirs. For the French and the other participating nations, it ensured that no European state (read Germany) could go alone toward rearmament and that economic growth would be spread across all of Europe. This construction lasted until the mid-1980s. Enormously successful, it ensured peace and stability and promoted growth and employment. Very few people would contest the statement that this European organization started to fall apart in the late 1980s. At the end of the 1980s and especially at the turn of the decade it was abundantly clear that this construction had come to the end of its life. Its demise was illustrated by four main changes.

The breakup of the Soviet empire. This empire was an ideological empire with a common ideology linking people, nations, and ethnic minorities without any other common denominator. The ideology was imposed from above and openly or secretly opposed from below. When it became clear that the ideology did not provide any useful guidance for the problems of modern society but, on the contrary, actually posed an obstacle— an almost insurmountable barrier—to the rapid transformation of society, the empire lost its raison d'être.

The breakup of the Russian empire. This was a traditional empire with one group of people imposing its will on less powerful nationalities on its periphery. For 500 years the Russian empire expanded slowly and steadily, but it did expand. Now the Russian population has lost its dynamism and its will to exercise power. The subdued nations, sensing this letdown, jumped on history's bandwagon so as not to lose momentum.

In a way it is not surprising that the two empires fell apart at the same time. They contained a built-in contradiction: The basic philosophy of the Soviet empire was equality among all nationalities; in the Russian empire, all were equal, but the Russians were more equal than the others.

The Western model has won the race with the Eastern model. This is a fact of life. The Western semicapitalist, democratic model has produced growth and welfare. The Eastern communist/socialist model has not. In two areas the socialist model should in principle have performed better than the semicapitalist model: protection of the environment and income distribution. But it did not.

In the former communist/socialist countries, large areas and many people have been the victims of ruthless butchering of the environment. The socialist/communist model treated the environment much worse than the semicapitalist model. Income distribution may have been more equal in the socialist/communist countries for a very large part of the population, but on a low level, while the so-called nomenclatura lived in luxury comparable to the best available in Western Europe.

The European Union has become an indisputable success. The European Union has established itself as the only workable framework for integration in Europe. It applies to agriculture, industry, and economic policies. Increasingly, it is also applicable to foreign and security policies and to such legal matters as immigration. Only a few years ago, many people could still discuss whether a community was the right framework for the Western European integration. In the beginning of the 1990s, very few people would dispute that the European Union is the one and only vehicle for a European integration pointing toward political and economic unity in Europe—not Western Europe, but Europe.

In Central and Eastern Europe the nationalities, the people, and the ethnic minorities have escaped from the cultural yoke exercised by the Soviet empire and the Russian empire. The crucial observation is that these people have rediscovered their own roots. Now they want to rebuild their own cultures which were subdued for so long by cultural imperialism from the outside. They want to shape their own identities, their own lifestyles, their own special and distinctive characters. To do so they concentrate on the two main foundations for an independent culture: language and religion. Their traditional languages were subdued by the Russian empire which imposed on them the Russian language. Their traditional religions were subdued by the Soviet empire which imposed a useless ideology to conquer the souls of the people. It failed utterly to do.

It is not surprising that this cultural revolution in Central and Eastern Europe took place at the end of the 1980s. The introduction of information technology paved the way for this cultural revolution. The information technology has brought about a total revolution with regard to dissemination of information and technology. It has made it impossible for a political regime to control what kind of information its citizens devour. As long as the printed letter was the vehicle for dissemination of information and knowledge, the regime could control the information available to the citizens. The Central and Eastern European regimes used this control to paint a totally false picture of the achievement of the communist ideology, the state of affairs in the national states, and economic growth and welfare.

One occasionally reads articles and comments by people who fear that information technology provides the power elite with a magnificent instrument for controlling the large mass of people. To our mind, that idea is wrong; it happens the other way round. The terrifying police states appeared in what we may term "the paper age," when people communicated by writing messages on pieces of paper. In these circumstances, it was easy for the power elite to control the dissemination of information. Fouché, Himmler, and Beria did exactly that and with great success. The Shah in Iran failed to do so because some clever people discovered the use of the tape cassette. Handy and easily hidden from the Shah's secret police (Savak), the cassette could be used to disseminate information. In fact, it was a deadly weapon in the age of information especially in the hands of people with a firm belief in their religion wishing to control the population by using religion. The regimes in the former communist world could not continue to control the use of information because information technology broke their monopoly. Information technology liberates people and takes control away from regimes.

The regimes in Central and Eastern Europe were not only far off the mark but totally misleading to say the least. To speak quite bluntly: The regimes were for decades lying outright to their citizens. They got away with it for a long time because the old-fashioned dissemination of information and knowledge made it possible. When this was no longer the case, the populations quickly came to the conclusion that the power elite had lied purposely, continuously, and unscrupulously. This led to a complete breakdown of any confidence that might have existed between the power elite and the population. That is why it was so easy to tumble the regimes and why there was so little resistance. People never forget if the power elite lies.

To a certain degree, the same development could be traced in the periphery of the Soviet Union where people had access to information from outside. The information technology also played a major role in preventing the coup in Moscow in August 1991 from succeeding. The whole world watched Boris Yeltsin climb a tank and talk with the crew sent to bully him and his supporters into submission. Those pictures sent an electric shock throughout the world. At the same time it gave Yeltsin's supporters the feeling that their course and their fate was an international issue, not only a Soviet/Russian question. Their destiny was being watched by the whole world. They knew it, and it gave them strength. The coup makers also knew it, and it terrified them paralyzing their will of action at a crucial moment. The contrast to East Berlin in 1953, Budapest in 1956, and Prague in 1968 is striking. In these cases, the Soviet system managed—not completely but to a large extent—to turn off the information channels. The rebellious forces felt that they were alone. That weakened their determination. That also strengthened the determination of the regime to use force.

The evolution taking place in Central and Eastern Europe is a clear-cut example of the two-sided effect of information technology. On the one hand, it globalizes dissemination of information and knowledge; on the other hand, it not only makes possible but also stimulates the drive for cultural decentralization. Globalization and localization go hand in hand. They do not contradict each other.

2

The Framework for a European Model

The European model of the future is based upon two fundamental principles: economic internationalization and cultural decentralization. In economic internationalization, policy making is transferred from the national state to the European (international) level. Cultural decentralization means that the evolution of culture, which takes place on a regional/local level, is not controlled and confined by the framework of the national state.

At first glance, these power shifts may appear to be incompatible because one goes one level up with regard to economic internationalization and one or two levels down with regard to culture. How would two such tendencies fit into a coherent model? In fact they do so very nicely. When we look farther into what happens, we will discover that they are not only compatible, they support each other. They are inseparable twins, two sides of the same coin.

Europe will teach the world how economic, industrial, and technological integration can be combined with cultural independence (cultural self-determination) for peoples, nations, and ethnic minorities. What is happening now in Europe is this great social experiment. It is the most spectacular one of its kind for more than two centuries. The framework is primarily the development toward political union and the economic and monetary union. In fact, these two unions are the vehicle for transforming economic internationalization and cultural decentralization into a workable European model. Parallel to these endeavors, we witness tremors in individual European national states which are trying to resist the onslaught of economic internationalization and cultural decentralization.

When we approach the end of the decade, not only will the political and economic architecture of Europe have changed substantially, even dramatically, but the social fabric of the individual national states will be far away from vintage 1989–1990.

The year 1991 will be recorded in history for bringing the concept of federalism to the forefront. This is the case for the three big political entities: The United States of America, the Soviet Union (as it was then), and Europe. The development in India is another illustration. And, of course, Yugoslavia. Federalism has been put on the political agenda, but the discussion and the political direction do not follow an identical pattern.

When U.S. President Bush presented his State of the Union Message in the beginning of 1991 most observers focused upon the section dealing with the war in the Persian Gulf. History will prove them wrong. The policy making in President Bush's statement touched on a totally different topic: the role of the federal government versus the individual states. What President Bush told his audience was that almost sixty years of uninterrupted centralization of power favoring the federal government to the detriment of the individual states should be reversed. The basic structure of the American society and the American political system was highlighted in that statement. The evolution started by Franklin D. Roosevelt was brought to an abrupt halt, and the engine was put in reverse gear.

Many states in the United States advertise their individuality, especially in the South where the link to the Latin culture is growing in the slipstream of immigration from Central and Latin America. The states themselves are the object of secessionist forces. For example, in California the northern third is considering breaking away from the rest of the state. In fact, such political movements were on the agenda in the beginning of the 1940s but were stopped by World War II. Now they surface again bringing into the open the fact that California as a state is not a homogeneous entity.

Canada shows a similar picture. Strong cultural forces work to disrupt the political unity. Many observers take the view that it is only a question of time before a large part of Canada will be engulfed by the United States. Quebec, as the odd man out, will have to make a living on its own or adjust to the fact of political and economic geography.

The heavily centralized system of the Soviet Union has been under attack from the inside for many years. The ideological yoke imposed upon almost every individual has been loosened. The centrally planned economy is being phased out. The individual republics have gained independence after a protracted political process lasting several years. A large part of more than 500 years of imperial policy by czarist Russia was lost in a few years' time (from 1989 to 1992). Instead of the once mighty Soviet Union, we have numerous independent republics. Russia itself is undergoing a change, not unlike the Turkish experiment, in the second decade of this century. The Turks were happy to dismantle the Ottoman empire because it had become a burden instead of an asset. Around 1990 the Russians came to the conclusion that the Soviet Union (Soviet empire) had become a burden instead of an asset. The Russians find the burden of empire as repulsive as the Turks did more than seventy years ago. Now, in the 1990s, however, the Turks are beginning to flirt with some of the old notions incorporated in the Ottoman empire. Apparently the Turks are not so convinced anymore that everything associated with their lost empire was as bad as it seemed at the beginning of this century.

The European Union is not a union in the original sense of the word nor is it a federation. It starts, so to speak, from the opposite end of the scale having to feel its way gradually and cautiously toward some kind of European union. Some people take the view that just when federalism is proving a failure in the United States and the Soviet Union, Europe is committing the fatal error of moving in the direction away from which these two political entities are moving. We do not agree with that view. It is much more simple. All three political entities approach some kind of common denominator, but they start from different points on the scale.

If we include other federations than those mentioned above (India, Yugoslavia, Canada, Australia, Myanmar) and confederations (Switzerland), we get a reasonably solid basis laying open what makes or undoes a federation: cultural imperialism or cultural independence. Before entering deeper into the topic, we would like to make it clear that, to our mind, culture is synonymous with the set of values governing the everyday life of the individual: what is good and what is bad.

We do not need to speak about federation here. Instead we can talk about the national state created in Europe during the last 200 years, most of which can be labeled artificial national states. These national states and the federations mentioned above would never have been able to survive as lasting political entities if they had tried to exercise cultural imperialism toward their regions, local communities, and individuals. Every time it has been tried, it has proved a failure with disastrous political consequences. Only when the national state or the federation has been wise enough to allow—even encourage—cultural liberty and cultural independence has the national state or the federation been able to survive as a viable political entity.

The lesson is simple. If one tries to harmonize culture as a set of values or to impose a certain set of values upon citizens resisting the idea, one will fail. During the industrial society and the industrial technology dominating the social fabric from the end of the 18th century to the end of the 20th century, many national states and federations managed to convince themselves and others as well that this could be done. They tried to put their stamp on history. But these efforts were in fact shadow boxing having little effect on the real thing. The introduction of information technology made it abundantly clear that any such attempt is doomed to failure. The mask has fallen.

The Maastricht Treaty respects this lesson. Its main characteristics can be summarized as follows:

1. It contains some *new principles for the integration started in 1952*. The most well known is the principle of subsidiarity pointing toward a distribution of competences among the community, the national state, and the regional level. Even if subsidiarity in its present form does not aim at a total recasting of the system, it may in the longer run have this effect. A lesson from history is that a cooperation or integration among national states reaches a point of no return when the distribution of competences between the national and international levels are handled.

2. The treaty falls into *two main parts*. The amendments to the existing treaties will take effect immediately after ratification of the Maastricht Treaty. These amendments are useful, but they do not really introduce any new basic elements. This can be said, however, about the other side of the coin—common foreign and security policy—including phrases on defense policy and defense, economic and monetary union, European citizenship, and legal cooperation. The treaty contains an ambition, a political objective that will have to be worked out and implemented at a later stage during the 1990s. To a large extent, what is new in the Maastricht Treaty has to be decided and fulfilled at a later date.

3. The Maastricht Treaty mirrors the *two strong tendencies* on European evolution for the next decades: economic internationalization and cultural decentralization. The treaty does not use these notions, but careful examination shows that it is indeed transforming these political tendencies into a treaty text. It is especially interesting to note that the Maastricht Treaty, contrary to the beliefs of many people, opens the door for decentralization and regionalization instead of centralization.

European evolution for the last 200 years has been turned around. Industrialization has run its course. The national state is being questioned. Centralization implemented or, shall we say, performed by the national state is being replaced by decentralization. In their graves so long forgotten, the Girondins of the great French Revolution must raise their heads if they had not been separated from their bodies by the guillotine. Was this not what they said and fought for? They lost their struggle then, but at last history vindicates their stance. In the years after 1789 the Jacobins, under the leadership of the ruthless Robespierre, won and wiped out their archenemies (the Girondins), the only people capable of posing a challenge. The Jacobins wanted centralization. That is what Europe got. In its extreme form, it led to such rulers as Hitler and Stalin. The wheel has turned. With luck we will see the Girondins of our age take over to introduce decentralization in Europe. The treaty is a child of its age. It was born exactly at the moment when Europe took off into the age based on information and knowledge.

The industrial age goes hand in hand with the well-known and artificial European national state—both developed during the last 200 years. In retrospect, the industrial age seems to be a step backward confining the horizon of the individual to a limited and narrow perspective. Before the beginning of the industrial age, the age of enlightenment ensured a broad perspective. The pacesetters did not limit themselves to specific sectors. They put their mind to the difficult but rewarding job of collecting data from various disciplines. Having done so they put these data together. Their picture of the world was not specialized, but it kept the mark of the generalists. Suffice it to mention Voltaire, John Locke, and David Hume.

The industrial age reversed this trend. Now every individual strove to stay within a well-defined and often narrow competence. After the beginning of the 19th century, it was rare to see philosophical works going beyond the knowledge of a specialist. People knowing every detail had the upper hand and they exploited it fully in digging deeply but not broadly.

The middle of the 20th century represents the pinnacle of this evolution. People's minds were confined to the national state and a one-language culture. People's insights were directed at a narrow technical or scientific segment. Science rarely transgressed national frontiers. The few attempts made at interdisciplinary endeavors were undertaken only with great difficulty.

The age of enlightenment was thus followed by the age of seclusion. The national state represented one side of this coin: seclusion from other national cultures and national identities confining people to think inside the framework of the artificial national state. The single-track disciplinary analysis forcing people to think in narrow terms represented the other side.

The evolution now taking place rejects this national seclusion. At the same time, it takes us toward a broader, much more "generalist" state of mind. In a way we are on our way toward a new age of enlightenment opening up our minds to new cultures beyond national borders and interdisciplinary analysis going beyond single-track science and technology.

3

Economic Internationalization

Under economic internationalization, almost all decisions concerning economic policy, monetary policy, industrial policy, and technological policy, as well as all the policies derived from them (e.g., transportation policy, environmental policy, and consumer protection) are transferred from the national level to the international level. In Europe that level is the European Union. The enterprises and the production factors (labor, physical capital, "money" capital, and, most important of all, knowledge) have already gone through this transition. National economic and industrial policies are illusions. Such policies are devoid of substance because the main factors—the enterprises and the production factors— have left the national straitjacket and are operating on the international (European) level. This reality is reflected in the plans for the economic and monetary union plus the European Union's much stronger impact in the areas of economic and industrial policies. No major enterprise can survive if its horizon is limited to national borders. It will die—quickly or slowly. The falling profit will squeeze it out of product development. It will be confined to producing traditional goods competing on prices with the inevitable result that the remuneration of labor and capital will fall. Such a vicious circle will quell even the most vital national enterprise.

The key to avoid this slow and agonizing death is to go international to maintain a foothold in the area of product development, product concept, quality, service, and design. This makes the enterprise visible for the group of consumers who are the pacesetters. This group changes constantly. It is never the same. There is only one common denominator: It is international. Linking up with this group of pacesetters enables the enterprise to discover the newest trends enabling it to market appropriate products and target a handsome price, boosting profits and remuneration of the production factors.

Because many of the well-known and well-tried buffer mechanisms of the industrial age have disappeared, economic systems react much more quickly to economic policy decisions than hitherto, although not in the way expected. Just-in-time production and just-in-time delivery means that stocks are negligible. The implication of this is a faster, more brutal reaction to upward pressure on the price level than we were accustomed to during the industrial age. We did not realize that because we have been living in an era of downward pressure on prices for the last decade; however, when the tide turns, we will all be surprised.

Another general impact of the economic internationalization is risk taking in a changed environment. Formerly, an enterprise knew that legislation was made by the national states and by them alone. Now legislation governing economic and industrial factors are gradually being transferred to international bodies. The implication is that enterprises need to evaluate the political environment and political development on the international level. A European enterprise simply must devote some resources to forecasting the future European integration. What shape will it take, which rules will be adopted, which policies are being implemented, and how will distribution of competences between the national and international level develop? Formerly, such questions were the prerogative of the national states themselves. Now these questions are just as much questions for the enterprises.

The future of a European enterprise might depend on whether it makes the right prognosis concerning technical standards and environmental protection, the policy of the commission with regard to competition, and state aid and rules concerning closer cooperation among enterprises in different member states. None of these questions can be answered without devoting resources to forecasting the course of European integration.

The enterprise is being pushed into something quite new: evaluation of political factors on the international level. A wrong guess may mean severe losses and, in worst cases, bankruptcy.

In a way, this is not so different from the role of the national state itself. Formerly, it could pass legislation without much concern about outside interference. Now the national state must take into consideration that it operates in a legal framework in which the European Union has competence. The national state and the European Commission may not necessarily have exactly the same interpretation of European Union legislation. Member states sometimes have to run a risk—the risk of being taken to court by the commission. But without readiness to run that risk a good deal of legislation comes to a halt. All in all, the internationalization calls for increased risk taking by the national states themselves and by the enterprises.

THE INTERNATIONAL PRODUCT

The international product has replaced the national product. All products are international. If one breaks down any product, one will discover that an increasing share of the value added comes from raw materials, semimanufactured goods, and production factors imported from abroad. A Boeing jet with European engines is just as European as American. An Airbus jet with American engines is just as American as European. Any firm trying to base itself on the concept of a national product will be left behind in the competitive race and relegated to a harmless and inefficient producer of conventional goods. A cost analysis made in 1994 will show decreasing share for labor and capital with an increasing share for knowledge compared to the industrial age in the mid-1950s. When a ship is delivered from one of the Danish shipyards, labor costs account for less than 10 percent of the total cost. The interpretation of this is that the less international production factors (labor and machinery) account for a smaller share of the total costs whereas the more international production factors (financing and knowledge) grasp a larger piece.

Everybody immediately recognizes the validity of this concept in the area of industry, but it is also true in agriculture and—especially—the service sector. In Europe primary products for processed foodstuffs are being transported across borders. That would have been unthinkable and impossible some years ago, but not today. Some European countries have food-processing industries that simply cannot survive without access to other countries' primary products. So, even the old agricultural sector has moved into an era where products are not any longer national but international.

The service sector contains the most international products of all. It is based upon the most international production factors of all: knowledge and information. Financial services, transport services, and communication, not to mention entertainment, are unthinkable inside a strictly national framework.

THE INTERNATIONAL MARKET

The international market has replaced the national market. The marketplace is international. An international set of sensors is indispensable to the production and marketing of the right product in the right market at the right time. The firm must be able to detect, comprehend, and assimilate changes in consumer preferences at the very moment they start, but the firm will not be able to do that if it is confined to the national market. Operation on an international scale is vital because twists in consumer preferences never take place in the same geographical location.

The speed of transmission is phenomenal. In the good old days it took years for a product or a new fashion to spread across the world. Today it can be done and is sometimes done in hours. Television conveys new thinking. The jumbo jet follows closely behind as second best with a time lag of just days.

The time available to book the profit has shrunk. The implication is that the well-managed enterprise having positioned itself to take advantage of new fashions can earn fantastic amounts in a very short time. The problem is, of course, that it costs a lot of money to position a company to do that and it is not always clear—far from it—which new fashions will hit the bull's-eye.

RESEARCH AND DEVELOPMENT

Product development (research and development) has for many years been at the very top of best-selling catchwords in the so-called science of management. There is no need to elaborate on it in this context, except for two new factors.

First, there is the time factor. The sequence of new products has risen with a speed of a patriot missile. Any firm participating in this game will have to perceive product development as a continuous process requiring financial and human resources. Any firm taking a nap in order to recharge its batteries for the next round will discover that it has been completely dropped from the race.

Second, there is access to the mass of talent. Product development can be successful only if a firm manages to collect different kinds of talent to shape a team. A firm that tries to collect such a team in a national context will fail. The only way ahead for a firm is to go international basing itself on international knowledge, researchers, and scientists of various nationalities.

The 1980s saw the emergence of just-in-time production and just-in-time delivery. The 1990s have already seen just-in-time research and development. It is simply too costly to develop a product if it is not marketable at once. Only a very few enterprises could survive the financial costs following the emergence of a product for which the market does not yet exist. One of the management skills called for in this decade is a fine-tuning of research and development to new trends in demand.

Another catchword is sustainable research and development. No enterprise can survive in the long run if it develops products as isolated articles. It must be able to sustain continued research and development efforts to follow up on successful products.

PRODUCT CONCEPT

In the industrial age, we looked at everything from the angle of production. The typical organization of the enterprise was designed around the input of raw materials, industrial processing, storage processes, and marketing and sales. There was very little communication or interaction among these activities in the enterprise. Not only were they secluded from each other, often they fought each other in interbureaucracy battles. The idea or notion of the consumer and the service demanded by the consumer did not appear in the mind of management staff or in the organization of the enterprise.

This way of thinking was, and is, not necessarily bad. The problem is that it is linked to processing of raw materials. That is no longer the pull factor in the economy. When dealing with knowledge industries and service industries, this way of thinking is detrimental to the effective working of the enterprise. At best, it leads to inefficient allocation of production factors. At worst, it leads to discontented customers who leave the enterprise to purchase—not industrial goods—but service somewhere else.

Many people have had the experience of receiving several letters the same day from their bank or insurance company informing them of changes in company policy: one letter for accounts for the first child, another for the second child, a third for their own account, and so on. All have the same message that interest rates have gone up or down. One letter for car insurance, another for house insurance, a third for fire insurance—all have the same message that the price has been increased. This way of conducting business simply will not work in the future. The enterprise will have to start from the needs of the customer to serve the customer regardless of the internal processes in the enterprise. In the example above it means one letter from the bank or the insurance company giving the customer the basic message.

The simple industrial product is out. It is being replaced by what we term product concept. Back in the 1920s Ford Motor Corporation was challenged by General Motors. They offered the Chevrolet in many colors. When Henry Ford was exhorted by his staff to do the same with the Model T, Ford replied, "Anyone can get a Model T in any color, provided that any color means black!" This reflects product thinking: In this firm, we produce a product; the customer can buy it or not. This is the basic philosophy of the industrial society. With the coming of the immaterial society, based on culture, knowledge, and information, the firms will have to offer a product concept based upon the total needs of the customer. The basic idea is to find out what the customer needs and provide it regardless of whether it is in conformity with the existing product line. Formerly, production technology had the upper hand in deciding the policy of the enterprise. The enterprise produced and marketed products that fell into line with the production technology. Most managers were engineers and production engineers at that.

This tendency is being reversed. Demand controls production. Enterprises not able to adapt their production technology to the needs of the market cannot compete efficiently. It is not a coincidence that this reversal of tendencies takes place at the moment when the industrial age is out and the information age is in.

The information technology will supplement purchasing power as the decisive factor when the consumer makes his or her choice. The fact that information technology broadens the horizon of the consumer to an extent not foreseeable means that what may be termed new consumerism will put production technology out of the picture as a determining factor. Before dealing in depth with the implication of product concept for new consumerism, let us cast a glance on its repercussions for investment goods. They are far-reaching, almost revolutionary.

It can be said in a very clear and unequivocal way: A few years from now investment goods incorporating new technology won't be sold unless accompanied by a total and comprehensive education and learning program. A signal system for railways will not be marketable unless the supplier offers simultaneously and as an element of the package, a comprehensive education and learning program for the people who are going to use the system. We can almost say that in this respect the staff is a consumer. Or in other words, to sell investment goods the enterprises need to master marketing of consumer goods. The program will make it possible for the railway staff to get used to the new technology without actually having to run the trains. They can learn what to do and how to react from the education program. For example, that can be done in China even if the signal system is produced in Germany. The system will ask for answers to problems such as an unexpected signal or a faster or slower train ahead of us than envisaged or problems at the next station. The result of the decision taken by the driver will be made completely clear showing whether the decision was the right one or whether it would have killed thirty-five people. The education and learning system will then also be a classification system telling which people are qualified to control our plant or our signal system.

Exactly the same goes for an air-traffic control system or a system to control reservations for tickets. The situation is analogous for an incineration plant. The staff can learn how to control the system before it is actually delivered. They can learn it anywhere in the world regardless of whether the plant is available. If problems arise the education system may tell whether that was due to too much wet waste, too much heavy waste, or a wrong method of input into the plant. It may go on to tell the operator what to do to remedy the mistake and to avoid repetition.

In the future what makes an investment plant sell may well be the quality of the accompanying education program more than the quality and performance of the plant itself. This will especially be the case when industrialized countries or countries moving from the industrial age into the information age are selling to newly industrialized countries or developing countries. In these circumstances the quality and accessibility of the education and learning program will be of paramount importance. The technology offered by various enterprises will be more or less the same. Consequently, it will diminish as competitive parameter. That place will be taken by education and learning programs.

Sometimes children can help adults to understand the idea of product concept. Children see things in a simple way. They look at what things are doing for them—which demands are being met. They do not care how and why things were made. Thus children start from the idea of basic needs when observing the surrounding world. Furthermore, children are obsessed by playing, which means that they have a broader view of things. They will often ask how they can use such a thing. Because they cannot read they do not look for the manual to find out what the thing was made for. A refrigerator is not a cold box but a box from which you get food. A chair is something you sit on. A ball is something you use to play. All subtle definitions are absent. We are back to the basics. That is where everybody should start to grasp what product concept really means.

To illustrate the notion of product concept, we would like to refer to the travel business. In the 1960s, Danish travel companies made a fortune out of introducing product concept. They offered cheap total packages to the Mediterranean seaside. Their philosophy was to take care of customers from their departure from the Copenhagen airport until their return two, three, or four weeks later. They offered satisfaction of the customer's total needs for leisure activity in a given period. That is product concept. A simple product would have been an air ticket and a hotel voucher. They did not offer travel; they offered leisure activities.

Another example can be found in the transport sector. In the 1950s, any shipping company would have shipped goods from the Copenhagen docks to New York harbor. That was their business. They did not care what happened before or after. There are no shipping companies left; instead, there are transport firms which pick up a container at a given address at a given time and deliver it at a certain time some weeks later at a certain address in Osaka, for example. The transport firms take care of the total transport demand of their customers. It is for this reason that most industrial activity is being spread around the globe. We find a certain amalgamation between industrial enterprises and transport firms. They cannot live without each other. The transport firms have grasped the idea of product concept and, by doing so, have carved out a very profitable business.

Environmental protection probably offers one of the shining product concept business sectors of the future. Today we look at this business in a compartmentalized way. We think of and speak of better water quality, less air pollution, and how to cope with an increased amount of solid waste—sometimes dangerous or even toxic. The point is that we look at it with industrialized glasses. We ask ourselves how we can reduce already existing pollution. Two major changes will win over our minds in the next decade.

The first change will be in our perception of pollution—from reducing it to preventing it. That calls for fundamental changes in plants and machinery. Engineers will be forced to design production plants in a way that means less pollution even if it also means higher production costs. This is another way to introduce taxes in the struggle against pollution.

The second change is more complicated. Governments and local communities will cease to talk about how to improve water quality and air quality and how to reduce solid waste. Instead they will call for a solution to improve total environmental quality, for example, by 25 percent in three years. Gradually they will abandon the sectoral approach and call for plans that encompass all three major vectors of environmental protection. The implication of this for the business sector is that firms specializing in one of these three vectors will find it increasingly difficult to prosper. Instead enterprises offering a package encompassing all three sectors will see market shares rise phenomenally. Of course, a medium solution is to make strategic alliances between enterprises in all three sectors, but that can be only a poor second best. We still have not got the environmental protection enterprise offering solutions in all areas but we will—soon. Some years from now it will not be uncommon to see local communities asking businesses to submit solutions for a certain percentage improvement in the environment.

Many of the facilities offered in Western Europe by the welfare state will slide into product concept. Health care is an example. We no longer speak about the number of hospital beds. We speak about health care—what can and should be done to improve total health care. It is not a question of hospitals or doctors or nurses or cost of medicine. What matters is how we can offer an improvement in health care delegating all these narrow sectors to their proper role as instruments to implement the objective. And how we can do it at an affordable price. The notion of costs will pave the way for product concept because we can achieve more for less money by basing ourselves on product concept instead of looking for improvements in secluded sectors of health care.

The health sector is, in fact, a very good illustration of the industrial angle versus product concept. In the 1950s people in a hospital were treated like an industrial good. They were the raw material being processed in the hospital which itself was a factory. They were received, stripped of their clothes, bathed, put into a bed, and then they waited for the operation or the treatment, lay in their beds to be examined by the doctors, and finally, after being declared fit for the market, were allowed to leave the hospital. This way of thinking is still valid in some places. That is where the health sector is really costly.

The product concept means that we start with the patient to find out, in cooperation with the patient, what the problem is and how it can be solved in a way that is acceptable to the patient. That may not necessarily be hospital treatment; other, less costly methods may be on the table. The heart of the matter is that the patient is no longer raw material for industrial processing but is demanding service and deciding the framework for this service.

Care for the elderly falls into the same category. We no longer speak about old-age homes. We try to mold together a total package to improve life for the elderly people in our society. Some of these facilities provide care for the elderly; others try to make it possible for the elderly to stay in their own homes longer with part-time assistance perhaps with the help of electronic gadgets.

Exactly the same approach can be seen with regard to children. Gradually we cease talking about nursing homes, preschool facilities, school, and supplementary facilities. Instead we look at it in the way that children shall be offered a whole range of opportunities for a long time span. In several of the most advanced societies, the step has been taken to break down the hitherto insurmountable barrier between play and schoolwork. In fact, the notion of play may take on a considerable role for the school system.

Finally, the protected home offers the same picture. Nobody is interested in a safe door lock. Everybody is looking for a home that is difficult for a burglar to enter. The door lock is not the solution. It is one of many instruments which combined offers the right solution.

The notion of product concept does not stop with the product itself. It will govern the restructuring of our industrial life, determine the use of technology, and put new emphasis on packing. Very few large and medium-sized enterprises are modeled to take advantage of product concept. That will change. In the future, the most successful enterprises will be those that are designed and structured to do exactly this. That is the case with numerous enterprises in the service and transport sectors. Many trading companies follow the same pattern. Their expansion especially with regard to strategic alliances and purchase of enterprises are designed to enlarge and deepen—at the same time—the concept they offer to the customer.

In the environmental field, we have yet to see the broad enterprise offering the total range, but we will soon discover that purchases of enterprises are being carried out to that purpose. This development poses a challenge and an opportunity for countries and enterprises. Many countries do actually possess some fairly advanced enterprises in the environmental field, but they do not cover all three sectors (air, water, and solid waste). The most advanced companies in one or two of these areas may be bought by companies in other countries. Superficially, that might not seem to be a bad idea. It may even be regarded as an advantage in the sense that, if one does not possess the necessary financial and human resources to further research and development, it makes no sense to stay in business. But, in the longer run, that means total abandonment of presence in this vital sector (environmental protection) because business will be made not by individual enterprises in each of the three sectors, but by enterprises encompassing all three and thus offering a product concept. The battle to be seen in the next five to ten years is about which enterprises and which countries will forge companies offering the total range. The same will be seen in health care, care for the elderly, care for children, and in several other sectors.

Acquisitions, mergers, and strategic alliances will be controlled by the idea of building a capacity to deliver a product concept instead of a product. The implication of this thinking is that the restructuring of industry will change. Until now most or almost all restructuring has aimed at making enterprises stronger where they already possess a production capacity (BMW and Rover, Asea and Brown Bovery, etc.). From now on the objective of most restructuring will be to shape enterprises or alliances combining different enterprises each offering something which taken together constitutes a product concept. Before, it was logical for a big enterprise cleaning water to purchase water-cleaning enterprises in other countries to build a strong base in this segment of the market. From now on, it will make sense for an enterprise with a strong base in air quality to buy a water-cleaning enterprise to move into product concept.

In the vocabulary of the industrial age, vertical integration between enterprises will be replaced by horizontal integration. It has been conventional wisdom for a number of years that the diversified enterprise was out. The thing to do was to concentrate on the one or two sectors in which the enterprise was already a strong competitor and stick with it. That may have been a wise tactic, but it will not continue to be so. In the future, only enterprises choosing the horizontal approach will be viable in the long run because it is only the horizontal approach that allows the enterprise to build a strong base with regard to product concept.

A good example of how well-known production technology has been used to make a new product is the Walkman. An even better example is the windmill. Denmark, without any basis whatsoever in the production of energy, is now a world leader in this field despite no prior Danish production technology in the area. The basic technology came from elsewhere, but the Danish producers put it together in a new way to make a windmill because they live in a country with strong winds. Almost everybody in the field of engineering could have done the same but did not because they were dominated by production managers. Again and again! Shift to look at it from the customers' angle—how to use the technology, not the other way around.

One of the most important strategic decisions is whether the enterprise is going to develop education and learning programs in-house or whether they will buy them outside. The horizontal approach tells us that in the long run, most enterprises will choose to control this very important competitive parameter themselves. Otherwise the enterprise offering these education programs can sell to its competitors. The problem is that very few investment goods enterprises are actually capable of granting the freedom required to develop these programs. It means that they will have to offer asylum so to speak, inside the firm, to people from a totally different culture. This is a challenge to management.

Packaging will play an ever increasing role. It is the window to the customer—the customers' first glimpse of the product. There are also several other and more intriguing reasons. First of all, the best package catches the eye and keeps the customer attached to the product. In a world of "pressure of impressions" that is extremely important. Second, protection of the environment means that packaging material should be recycled. That imposes a constraint on the kinds of materials that can be used. Third, the packaging needs to be inexpensive for those companies competing only on price not on quality and service. Fourth, as the population grows older, packaging must cater to the elderly by being easy to read and easy to open. Decades from now, it will not be possible to sell milk containers and glass bottles that require significant finger strength. Many elderly people have stiff fingers and suffer from arthritis, which leads them to ask for cans and bottles that can be opened easily. This may be the most neglected market niche of all.

LOCATION

In the industrial age, enterprises were linked to specific geographical locations. Information technology and the revolution in transportation systems have done away with such localization. Information technology has made it possible for a firm to coordinate operations internationally, even globally. Here we do not speak of subsidiaries of the same firm, but the distribution of different activities over a large geographical area regardless of political borders. The glue is provided by the emerging transportation companies which shuttle goods and products to and from the various entities of the same firm. The introduction of just-in-time delivery has been a milestone in the shaping of truly international and multinational firms.

The *Wall Street Journal* reported at the end of 1992 that Swissair was transferring its accounting department from Zurich to Bombay. The article noted that several other airlines were contemplating similar moves. This, in a nutshell, is the freedom to choose location. On closer inspection, it is not that localization has become irrelevant but that the criteria governing the choice of locale have changed completely. Some of these criteria are access to international networks for communication, access to a research and development environment, access to cultural stimuli, and environmental quality. Note that all these criteria have very little to do with hardware—buildings, plants, machinery.

If we look at the United States and Europe we find ample evidence to support this evolution. In the United States it is clear that the economic and industrial center has for some time been moving from the Northeast to the West and the South. Suddenly, one of the fastest growing states, in 1992, was Idaho. No one would have believed several years ago that such a development would take place. Again the freedom to locate shows remarkable and striking results. It underlines the tendency to decentralization. It is now possible to locate according to preferences, which have probably always been there but until now have been hidden away because it was not feasible or not profitable. People may always have liked to live and work in a clean environment with little or no noise. In the industrial age that was a dream. Now it can be done. And it is profitable to do so because people and not machinery are the principal production factor. People living in a stimulating environment produce more and better ideas than people living in the slums of the old industrial age.

In Europe the old industrial regions are taking on the role of underdeveloped regions. That is true of areas in Britain, Germany, France, and Spain. In all these countries, the center of gravity is moving from where it used to be to new geographical areas. In Germany it is Baden-Württemberg. In France it is the south. In Britain it is the south and west. The newest example is Sweden—once a model industrial country—now in a difficult economic situation, and it is most clearly seen in the old industrial centers in mid-Sweden.

In a more general context it can be said that the transition from industrial to immaterial society means that territory as a notion loses importance. In the hunter, agricultural, and industrial societies, economic and cultural activities were linked to territory. Power and influence were dependent on access to and dominance of territory. This is no longer so. Territory is less important than knowledge and information.

Indeed, this development is one of several factors behind the problem of the national state. The national state is based upon the idea of territory. If or when territory loses its importance so does the national state.

Freedom to choose location for enterprises and the gradual decline of the national state thus have a common denominator: the phasing out of territory as a parameter in the power (economic and political) game. We will elaborate on this idea in chapters 4, 5, and 6.

HUMAN RESOURCES

Human resources and human capital outshine physical capital (plants). Formerly enterprises were interested in the production technology in the form of machinery. Now the focus is on human resources. What an enterprises buys when it takes over another enterprise is not the machinery and the buildings, it is the human resources assembled in that particular enterprise. Competitiveness is controlled by human capital.

For many years statistics have shown something strange. Productivity does not grow immediately after investment. The explanation is easy to find. The new equipment could be used only after the staff had been trained and educated. It took a few years, only after which did productivity start to grow.

New equipment in the modern enterprise is very costly. It is not like the old days when an enterprise just bought a new machine from time to time. Today most investments are carefully planned to fit into production, delivery, research and development. The implication of this is that such equipment must not be unused. It has to be operating most of the time. For this reason, service plays an increasing role for competitiveness. If an enterprise can guarantee that any problem with the machinery it has delivered will be solved within two or three hours, it will make sense for companies to buy that equipment even if it is more expensive than competing equipment.

At the same time, this means that enterprises will have to plough a considerable amount of money into training their staffs. The company simply cannot afford to have workers or staff damaging expensive machinery stopping production and making it necessary to undertake costly repairs. What really matters in this context is the risk of being unable to deliver, thus falling off the wagon entitled just-in-time delivery. Only a well-trained and highly professional staff can live up to these expectations.

This is one reason behind support for the social dimension of the European Community. It improves working conditions thereby associating workers and staff more closely to the enterprise making it more likely that they will understand the need for skills and see it in the context of the three just-in-times (JITs).

Competition today is so intense that an enterprise cannot operate within a framework permitting more than one idea of strategic importance to be tried. The financial resources are not available. Management has to come up with the single strategy that is the right one at the right moment. Years ago, several ideas could be tried and the winner picked from this competition. An enterprise trying that today would go bankrupt. What has been stated here applies to strategy. With regard to tactics, it is the other way around. On this level, many ideas should be floated and tried. The good one or ones could then be picked. Here it would be a disaster to have only one idea.

Strategy in both its military and competitive meanings is the ability to position one's own forces according to one's own choice while at the same time denying that possibility to one's enemy. During World War II, Hitler did not realize that by closing the Mediterranean to the Allies he would impose an almost intolerable strain on their shipping tonnage. Field Marshal Alan Brooke (chairman of the British Joint Chiefs of Staff) saw that by sweeping the Axis forces clear of the south side of the Mediterranean the tonnage gain would tremendously increase the freedom to maneuvre of the Allies. A good strategy in business was to concentrate on container transport with delivery at scheduled times exactly at the moment when just-in-time delivery conquered industrial production.

Tactics in both its military and competitive meanings is the ability to concentrate one's own forces at the right spot while forcing the enemy to disperse his forces. The German attack in May 1940 through the Ardennes against a French army spread out over the whole of northern France demonstrates this point.

The marketing of a brand name in, for example, the beer market aiming at high quality falls in the same category of well-applied tactics provided that it is being done with sufficient determination. The opposite of such a tactic is to aim at various segments of the market thus blurring the identity of the product in the eye of the customer. Its uniqueness gone, a brand name is not worth a penny.

COMPETITION

Competition has become tougher and will continue to do so. In the 1980s competition was a soft pillow compared with the fakir bed of the 1990s. Competition will be fierce, ruthless, and bloody. Not only that, it will be much more complicated. In the good old days of the industrial age with the product in focus all that mattered was low cost. Squeezing the costs increased the market share. With the coming of the immaterial society and the product concept this approach is a nonstarter. The single-string competitive game will be replaced by a multi-string composed of several competitive parameters: costs, product concept, product technology, quality, service, and design. And do not forget the three JITs. Perhaps the most decisive change for investment goods is the linkage between the plant itself and the accompanying education and learning program. Those enterprises grasping this new phenomenon may be the pacesetters of the future.

The challenge to management is to put together the right mix of these parameters at a given time in a given market. As demand changes constantly, management will have to adjust constantly the composition of the competitive parameters. It is imperative to change the composition of competitive parameters over time, but management will also have to put emphasis on different parameters in different markets. It may be an idea to focus on design in Japan, quality in the United States, and technology in Europe. Even if product concept is the same, it is not exactly the same in different markets, and it will have to be marketed with emphasis on various characteristics according to the marketplace in question.

Marketing people will have to understand that instant impressions play a significant role in the choices made by consumers. Packaging and presentation win an ever increasing role because they first catch the eye of the consumer. The supply is so overwhelming that consumers face a kind of pressure of impression.

The key to understanding what may be termed new consumerism is that this is going to be not only consumption but also entertainment. People shop and buy where they find entertainment and entertaining goods. Shopping is no longer an exclusive economic activity. It is going to be more and more of a cultural activity where the consumer craves something more than just the goods offered. The shop will gradually be changed into a small unit for entertainment competing with TV and other cultural activities. The goods themselves will increasingly be marketed and sold on the basis of noneconomic factors, and they need to attract the attention of the consumer instantly and without giving pause for reflection—for the simple reason that such reflection may be used for consideration of other goods.

The difficult thing to grasp is that this goes hand in hand with another, much more boring kind of shopping: low-cost shopping where everything has to be offered at the lowest possible price. There is no service, no facilities for repair or maintenance, but long lines at the cashier. The concept is that the consumer pays a low price and gets what he or she paid for. In this sector absolutely no entertainment is associated with shopping. In this category we find everyday shopping (e.g., food and beverages).

A CULTURAL PROFILE

Let us go one step farther in analyzing the competitive game. During the 1990s, culture will gradually take over from economic and techno-logical factors as the decisive instrument for winning the great game. Well-run companies have developed a company culture—an esprit de corps—but that kind of company culture was linked to the firm's activities and did not have much to do with the development of culture in society—what we term the set of values controlling the development of society. That is why the well-known concept of company culture will no longer be sufficient. It must be supplemented or even replaced by what we term a cultural profile of the firm. That cultural profile needs to be communicated to three groups of people: customers, competitors, and the staff.

Customers

The implication of the immaterial society and culture as a pivot for the changing fabric of society is less an economic and more a value-orientated relationship between the customer and the firm. Formerly, the customer made his or her decision based on price and quality. This was a typical pattern in the product-orientated industrial society. In the fu-ture, customers will increasingly choose product concepts and select firms on the basis of the set of values chosen by the firm as the backbone of its cultural profile. This will occur in a very specific, well-defined way. Take environmental protection as an example. No firm can survive in the 1990s without following suit with regard to environmental protec-tion. But it goes much farther. The individual customer will expect a cultural profile in the sense of a set of values, and if the values are congruous that particular firm will be chosen.

The economic relationship between a customer and a firm is not stable. It can and will be discontinued if the economic parameters change. The cultural relationship is more stable because cultural parameters change much more slowly. Thus, by changing track toward a cultural profile as a first-rate competitive parameter, the firm will—if successful—achieve the fidelity of its customers. This observation can be confirmed by look-ing back on firms that have succeeded in selling their products as a lifestyle. What is new about this is the possibility of exploiting cultures as a set of values as the main competitive parameter. If such a strategy is to be crowned with success, the firm must not be quiet but, on the contrary, must make sure that its message is stated on the screen, in big letters. The firm must get its message across; otherwise, even the best cultural profile will not help. It is a death warrant to act like the old Danish proverb, "Those who live a quiet life, live a good life."

Let us consider a few examples. The Italian textile company Benetton has sported eye-catching advertisements in international newspapers. One would expect a textile company to focus on textiles or clothing, but Benetton has chosen a totally different approach. The advertisements show boat refugees, hunger-stricken people, and blood-stained clothes. The idea behind this approach is to use ethics as a breakthrough to the mind of the consumer. Benetton conveys the impression that it cares for these people, and if the customer also cares (and who does not?) the right thing to do is to buy products from Benetton. Who does not re-member the "United Colors of Benetton" with children from various races wearing brightly colored Benetton clothes. Again, the idea is to catch the mind of the consumer by saying that people with no racial prejudices (and who has them?) should buy products from Benetton.

The Body Shop, a British cosmetics company, has made it known that a part of its profits is allocated to development purposes in the less developed areas of the world so that the consumer feels that he or she is supporting development in poorer parts of the world. The objective is to reach out not necessarily to the mind of the consumer but to the conscience. The Body Shop is also known for selling products manufac-tured without animal testing. The customer buying these products does not need to have a guilty conscience; on the contrary, the customer has a clear conscience because each purchase, as a side effect, hits those cos-metic companies that are selling products based on the use of animal testing.

Competitors

The second target is the competitors: A company must mark its ter-ritory—exactly like the dachshund that does nothing else during the eve-ning walk. When following a competitive strategy based upon economic and technological factors, it is necessary to hold one's cards close to one's chest. But when one enters the great game, one must do exactly the opposite. The strategy must be brought out into the open so that one's competitors can see—in fact, cannot avoid seeing—what one has chosen as a cultural profile. Only by doing that can one prevent a competitive war by mistake. Because the competitive wars of the 1990s will be bloody wars, if it is necessary to enter a competitive war be sure that it is una-voidable and that it is fought on your terms. It goes without saying that it is difficult for a competitor to break up a stable customer-firm rela-tionship. In fact, we have a situation not unlike the nuclear deterrence of the Cold War period where the superpowers took great care to let their adversaries know the size of their nuclear arsenals.

The Staff

The third group, the most important group, is the staff. The staff is the firm vis-à-vis the customers and the soldiers vis-à-vis the competitors. A lot of effort may be devoted to designing a cultural profile since it is not an easy task; however, the real difficulty comes in communicating the profile to every single member of the staff and making sure that each one has fully understood it in its entirety. Communication has always been difficult. In the great game of the 1990s, however, it is a question of survival. If the members of the staff do not understand the cultural profile, they will be out of touch when problems confront them, and they may make the wrong decisions.

To illustrate this we would like to recall what the Romans did 2,000 years ago when they nominated a governor to their distant provinces. A governor in Britannicum who wrote, "I am being attacked. What should I do?" and waited six months to receive an answer, "Defend yourself" no doubt he would have been killed in the meantime. Pontius Pilatus had to solve a hideous problem in a way which to him conformed to the interests of Rome.

The Romans made sure that, before a governor left, he had held every possible position in Rome—censor, questor, and so on. By the time he had been through all the administrative branches of the Roman empire, he had written into his soul how a true Roman behaves. He knew how to act without instructions. Pontius Pilatus made the right decision from the point of view of Rome. The objective was to keep Palestine quiet. We know that his decision was, in fact, not the one he himself favored. The company culture of the ancient Roman empire was strong enough to conquer the conscience of Pontius Pilatus.

In today's world, distance is no longer a problem, but two new impediments have arisen. The first one is time. There is no time to consider what to do. Staff members must react by instinct; otherwise, competitors will get in and conquer. The second impediment is the incredible amount of information masking the indispensable bit of information needed immediately. The manager and staff members must go through this phenomenal amount of information and pick without hesitation what is needed here and now. Years ago, there were people called "skimmers" who went through newspapers and within minutes, or even seconds, could pick out exactly what was needed. This magic touch is needed more than anything else in the information age.

The ability to act on the spot in conformity with the company culture and the cultural profile of the firm is the key to solving these problems.

Again, the essential factor is to make the cultural profile as clear and visible as possible. Do not spare any effort to make it known to every individual in the firm which set of values has been chosen by the firm. There are many ways to do this. Pride is the key. Some of the best company cultures can be found in the regiments of the British army. Look at their uniforms. There are colors and battle records. They are proud of their performance. A well-run firm with sufficient profit can build upon pride in the same way.

The shift in competition from economic parameters to a cultural profile means a shift away from plant and machinery toward the staff, that is, toward human resources management. It is not enough to depend on management in the illusory hope that a few top managers can do the trick. They cannot. It is necessary to get through to the staff as a whole with a clear message about the firm's policy and its cultural profile. The rapid shifts in product development, production methods, and marketing mean that most decisions must be made on the spot—not by management, but by the staff. If not, the firm falls behind and will not be able to stage a comeback without luck, and it is dangerous to rely on the capriciousness of luck. The staff can make quick decisions only if they know exactly what the firm stands for, what its policy is, what its objectives are, and what means are the chosen ones to achieve other objectives. That is the framework for the staff and for the decisions they make. The task for management is to provide that framework and then to communicate it constantly to the staff.

It is quite evident that many firms, especially in the United States but also in Europe, have not, far from it, grasped this essential shift. They still regard the staff (labor force) as a somewhat unavoidable nuisance which constitutes a problem because they are not ready to accept the low wage afforded by management. Such an attitude scares away the most important asset of the firm, the employees.

Field Marshal Montgomery was an excellent communicator. He managed to convince his soldiers that everything would go according to plan even if it never did. His strong impact on the rank and file made the soldiers do even more than he expected. From August to October 1942, in the Western Desert, Montgomery used persuasion and personal appearance to mold a rather disillusioned army into a high-quality fighting force. Before his great battles, he always talked to his officers and used the opportunity to be seen by as many troops as possible. He became a person most soldiers had seen, not merely a name or a picture. His use of simple signals, such as his black tank beret, was an outstanding success. In fact, he was more a manager than a soldier.

The military does indeed provide some of the best examples of company culture and cultural profile. The policy is made clearly visible very quickly. It is difficult to hide mistakes. Soldiers and officers communicate their attitudes toward the leadership. Their contempt or admiration penetrates any mist. Appearance cannot hide realities. During World War II it was said of one of Montgomery's predecessors that he had a great air of decisiveness about him but was, in fact, very indecisive.

The military brings out into the open an essential idea: keep it simple stupid (KISS), which was invented by the American army during World War II. Simple and easily understood guidelines for action can be followed by soldiers even under stress; complicated guidelines containing several messages cannot.

Apparently, the secret lies in finding the exact keyword that corresponds to the cultural profile chosen. It may be better service, faster service, better design, punctuality, technology, forward planning, or one of many others. It is not good to choose several keywords because it messes up the message. The staff needs one parameter, not several which may from time to time contradict each other.

The firm and its staff should then take pride in performing better than their competitors as stated in the chosen keyword. Not the management but the staff should regard it as a major problem if delivery is late for a firm having chosen "always punctual" as its keyword. The staff should on its own initiative report it to the management accompanied by a report of why it happened and which precautions have been taken to avoid a repetition. When the staff become aware of increasing revenues and increasing profits, pride will grow.

Pride in doing something better than other people is understood by the military but not always by business. All this can be done in small and medium-sized enterprises—those which will prosper in the future—but it cannot be done in enterprises with a staff of several hundred thousands. These enterprises are really too big and too cumbersome to forge and maintain a cultural profile. It is not possible to get across to so many people.

The question is what will happen to the big monoliths constructed during the final decades of the industrial age and the first decades of the immaterial age. The answer is that either they will wither away or they will decentralize. The real question, however, is what is meant by decentralization in an age dominated by culture as the competitive parameter and the cultural profile of the enterprise as the cornerstone for the policy inside the enterprise.

Hitherto, decentralization has been carried out in several ways. Enterprises have, for example, decentralized by making profit centers. That solution is good, but it is not good enough. A decentralized profit center is based upon an economic concept and not on a cultural concept. To do that we need to decentralize culturally. Many big enterprises will have to encourage guerilla activities inside the firm to challenge the dominant culture; otherwise, the dominant culture will rest on its laurels until it discovers that other enterprises have overtaken it—and then it is too late. Management may find that difficult to do because it means higher costs in the initial phase.

More generally, big enterprises will have to decentralize culturally. In practice, that will mean two things. First, there may be a clash between the cultural profile of the enterprise and the regional or local culture. Experience indicates that a cultural profile cannot be implemented in other cultures without some adjustments. The regional or local culture may itself provide an input to the cultural profile. The more an enterprise understands this, the more it can gain from cultural encounters all over the world. The less it understands, the more centralized and more useless the cultural profile will become. The interaction between a cultural profile and many different regional or local cultures may become a strong asset for an enterprise. The worst of all cases is a clash between the cultural profile and the regional or local culture; nevertheless, many enterprises experience this difficulty.

Second, the enterprise should allow several cultures inside the firm to compete among themselves. Some activities of the enterprises may be linked to a culture emphasizing quality. Other activities may be linked to a culture based upon punctuality. And some other activities may be linked to low prices. That may sound a little bit odd and even give rise to some suspicion about a confused message. In the future, however, many of the activities inside an enterprise will look rather confused. That is unavoidable when we change from the strict technology and economic control of the industrial age to the immaterial society based on culture and ideas. The challenge is to combine the two: to get several cultures inside the enterprise to promote new ideas while at the same time managing the economic activities of the enterprise in an old-fashioned way. Whether this is a new discovery is debatable, but the priority among these parameters has been switched. In the industrial enterprise, priority was given to economic control; in the immaterial society, it will be the other way around.

It is difficult to escape the conclusion that not many of our present-day big enterprises will be able to survive those challenges without deep and profound scars.

One idea of how to cope with this problem can be found by looking closer at the esprit de corps in army regiments during peacetime versus during wartime. The army or army corps for that matter is a loose unit that does not really exist during peacetime. If it does it is ordinarily for administrative purposes. The regiments, however, are the stable units that gather soldiers during peace and war and mold them into real soldiers. The regiment is based upon tradition, and well-known catchwords are communicated to and respected by all members of the regiment— recruits as well as veterans. Everyone knows all the battles the regiment has fought and its battle honors. The regiment is, so to speak, a world in itself. It can be moved from one army to another. It will still be the same regiment. It will still have the same esprit de corps. The core of the army is the regiment because wherever it is posted it will be the same unit with the same qualities.

The army, however, is ephemeral. It will not exist beyond the time required to fight a war, which will be short compared with the centuries of existence of which some regiments can boast. The army takes on its own life only after several successful battles, for example, the German Afrika Corps and the British Eighth Army which fought against each other in the Western Desert during World War II. The same can be said of the U.S. Third Army during the campaign in northwestern Europe from July 1944 to May 1945. The implication is clear enough. The army gathers its esprit de corps from victories. If there are no victories, there is no esprit de corps. One victory is not enough. The regiment gathers its esprit de corps from decades or centuries of fighting, which results in traditions, sometimes associated with defeat but, in that case, an honorable one.

The following lessons can be drawn. The regiments represent many different cultures, but they are nevertheless employed together. They are being used according to their comparative advantage. They all strive to achieve one common and well-defined objective. The organization is loose and temporary. When the objective is achieved, the organization (the army) is dissolved. The regiments are not. They are sent elsewhere to achieve another objective. All these lessons can be learned from military history. They can be used by today's enterprises free of charge. The regiments are integrated in a common endeavor without losing their cultural profiles. They mix but do not combine.

4

Cultural Decentralization

The foundation for this communication to the staff of the cultural profile of the firm is a clear perception of the cultural battle to take place in Europe during the 1990s. There will be four main actors: the global mass culture, the regional or local culture, the national state, and the enterprises or trade unions.

THE GLOBAL MASS CULTURE

The global mass culture is an American-inspired culture. An audio-visual culture, its vehicles for communication are pictures, symbols, and logos. To a large extent, it is interwoven with the concept of Hollywood. It took off in the 1920s with the comic strip when, for the first time in history, text and pictures were linked to communicate a message. Gradually, pictures have taken over as the dominating factor; for example, in international airports, pictures have replaced text as guides for world travelers.

The best illustration of this global mass culture is the television news network CNN. CNN is for adults what comic strips are for children. The viewer is presented with a continuous stream of information cut into thirty-second reports. It shifts from one subject to another with phenomenal speed. It is flicker. It is a pressure of impressions with an overwhelming impact on the individual. The viewer's main problem is to transfer impressions received on the TV screen to his or her own mental screen. The viewer gets a few seconds to decide whether he or she wants to do that. But the viewer is not able to stop the stream of information to deepen his or her insight into any one of the many items. The viewer is in the hands of the medium. The fight among all these impressions to get through to one's mental screen is devastating. It puts a strong pressure on the viewer to select and we are back to square one in the sense that the viewer is exposed to a stressful decision-making situation.

This occurs because not all of this flicker is accompanied by a firm and durable set of values. The lack of this cultural backbone makes it extremely difficult for the individual not only to select, but also to take positions vis-à-vis the impressions presented to him or her. In other words, the lack of a firm set of values increases the stress factor. To solve this problem, the individual looks for help. Where does one find a firm set of values that will provide the framework needed to survive the onslaught of the global mass culture?

THE REGIONAL/LOCAL CULTURE

Many Europeans find this framework in their own regional or local culture. The basic culture provides a handle, making it possible to resist the assault made on the soul by the storm troopers of the global mass culture.

The basic culture is communicated by means of language and religion. These form two strong pillars. They are not very malleable, at least in the short run. Furthermore, they are always accompanied by a firm and well-proven set of values which have survived decades, even centuries, of cultural attack. History shows again and again that the regional or local basic culture in Europe possesses tremendous staying power. These cultures can be traced back through the ages to their distant roots in the Roman empire. That is why we speak of basic culture. For centuries, these basic cultures have provided a safe haven for Europeans through turbulent times.

The Western world has seen two ideological empires: the Soviet empire, with a duration of seventy-four years, and the Catholic Church, which has survived for more than 1,700 years and is still going strong. Stalin made many mistakes. One of them was his assault against the other ideological empire in the Soviet heartland, that is Central and Eastern Europe, one of the strongholds of the Catholic Church. Stalin lost. This example illustrates the weight of the basic culture. Not even the "evil empire" could conquer its bastions, even if it had the fortune of following in the footsteps of another evil, authoritarian empire—the Nazis.

When one travels around Europe today, one often sees two flags: the flag of the region and the flag of the European Union. It may be necessary to go to an official building to glimpse the national flag. When the Olympic Games were broadcast from Albertville, the noticeable flag was the red-and-white flag of Savoy, which had a more prominent place than the tricolor of France.

In the United Kingdom, one of the themes in the election held on April 9, 1992, turned around Scottish home rule. The percentage of votes going to the Scottish national party is a threat to the established political parties, although it was lower than expected in April 1992. What about Wales? What about Ireland and the Gaelic/Irish language taking gradually over from English?

During the Olympic summer games of 1992, held in Barcelona, advertisements in many newspapers emphasized that the Olympic summer games were taking place in Barcelona, the capital of Catalonia, not a city in the country of Spain. The point here is that it did not say a region or a province in Spain.

During the regional elections held in spring 1992, the Catalan voter was confronted with the question of whether Spanish should continue to be the primary foreign language in Catalonia. The regional language is a strong pillar in the effort undertaken by Catalonia. Ninety-four percent of the population in Catalonia (6 million people) understand Catalonian; 69 percent can speak it; 40 percent can write it. The University of Barcelona offers two-thirds of its education in the Catalan language. The overwhelming number of books and examinations are in the Catalan language.

The cultural map of Spain is still marked by the cultural line drawn by the expansion of the Moors and the Christian principalities. Catalonia, Andalucía, Galicia, and the Basque country are all trying to escape the control exercised by the central government in Madrid. Similar are the distinctions between north and south in Italy, between Wallonia and Flanders in Belgium, and of course, the artificial national borders in Yugoslavia.

On the other hand, we have the Federal Republic of Germany and, to a certain extent, France. Germany is a very decentralized nation-state. Former Ministerpräsident Bjørn Engholm of Schleswig-Holstein has stated that in today's Germany many Germans feel a stronger cultural link to the *Länder* than to the federal state of Germany. When Germany negotiates in the European Union, the German delegation includes a representative of the *Länder*.

In 1969 Charles de Gaulle lost a referendum in France on the topic of decentralization and regionalization. In 1983 and 1986 President François Mitterrand introduced far-reaching legislation to that effect. The French referendum held in September 1992 on the Treaty of the European Union gave a slim majority of yes votes. However, the yes majority was much stronger in the peripheral parts of France. The interpretation is that these areas (regions/departments) saw the treaty as a lever to get more independence vis-à-vis Paris.

This explains why Germany and France do not fear a decentralized European political union. Its political system is geared to exactly that kind of government. The United Kingdom does possess that fear because its political system is geared to exactly the opposite. All powers are vested in Parliament, and it does not want to surrender any power at all whether it is to the European Union or to the local communities in Britain.

There is a very good reason why cultural decentralization with the regions as its pivot is taking place now. Formerly, the national state could and did threaten the regions with economic sanctions if they dared to leave the national state. Without participation in the economic life of the national state, which was a key to participation in the international economy, no region could survive. The idea of leaving the national state never survived the threat from the national state. In the 1990s, however, the European national state is no longer able to exercise a credible threat. Access to the international economy is no longer guaranteed by the national state, but by the European Union. And the union has no intention of giving the national state a helping hand to suppress cultural decentralization. That is why Slovenia dared to leave Yugoslavia, knowing that the European Union would provide them with access to the international economy. They had watched the European Union negotiate association agreements with Poland, Czechoslovakia, and Hungary, and they knew that the European Union had started negotiations about trade agreements with the three Baltic states that seceded from the Soviet Union.

This leads us to a very pertinent observation. Economic internationalization and cultural decentralization do not contradict each other; on the contrary, they go hand in hand. To put it in another way, economic internationalization is paving the way for cultural decentralization, which, in other circumstances, would be unthinkable and unfeasible. The European Union is the battering ram for cultural decentralization.

Not only are the regions back on the front page, we can observe a new concept: the cross-border region. This is a really new development. And it will change Europe's political and economic geography. Right in the heart of Western Europe, the old dukedom of Burgundy has reappeared. It encompasses some parts of France, some parts of Germany, and some parts of Belgium and Luxembourg. In the southern part of France, what nearly became a kingdom 800 years ago has begun to put its mark on the development: Occitania. Around Denmark we can see Schleswig-Holstein draw closer to Denmark, while Skåne in Sweden does the same. In the north of Europe, the Same-people of Norway, Sweden, Finland, and Russia have established a cross-border cooperation.

One of the biggest cross-border regions is to be found on both sides of the Pyrenees, the mountains separating France from Spain. The Spanish region of Catalonia is the driving force behind this enterprise that encompasses four Spanish regions (Catalonia, Aragon, Navarra, and the Basque country) and three French regions (Languedoc, Midi-Pyrenees, and Aquitaine) plus the small state of Andorra. Vienna-Budapest-Prague form a triangle constituting the center point in a cross-border region recalling Austria-Hungary before World War I.

Many of these names of regions are well known in history. They existed as political entities some centuries ago, but the coming of industrial Europe wiped them off the map. Now they have come to the surface again. Old and still existing links have gotten a renaissance. They were thought to be forgotten, but they are not. They are able to shape history once again because they are based upon culture, identity, and traditions in an era when the industrial society is being replaced by the information age.

The cross-border regions are one of the strongest forces that are breaking up the national state from within because they remove much of the power of the capital of the European national state. Formerly, it made sense to put a headquarters in Paris, when a foreign firm wanted to establish itself in France. From there, all France could be covered. That thinking is no longer valid. It is much better to establish a regional headquarters in one of the cross-border regions to benefit early from this new development. Thus the capital loses its grip on the economic and financial life of the national state. In today's Europe there is strong competition among a few centers to assume the role of the European financial center. That is obvious. But it less obvious that some smaller regional financial centers are growing to take responsibility for a region or a cross-border region.

During the 1990s we will see such cities as Copenhagen, Hamburg, Stuttgart, München, Milano, Barcelona, Lyon, and Toulouse take on another and much more important role: some as regional centers; others as centers for cross-border regions. Lyon may be quite important in a large part of eastern France, some part of Switzerland, and southwestern Germany. Copenhagen may get a role in a Baltic region. Hamburg may see the revival of its old role as a port for large parts of Central and Eastern Europe.

There is no doubt that the regions inside the existing national states may get not only a cultural and social role but also a political role. It is, however, an unanswered question as to whether the cross-border regions will be able to go beyond cultural and social affairs and move into politics. It is much harder and requires the breaking down of barriers. With luck, the European Union may play a role in this process and provide some help.

THE NATIONAL STATE

The artificial national state is being squeezed from two sides. Economic internationalization removes much of its economic and industrial policies by transferring powers to the European Union. Cultural decentralization means that people are transforming their identity and thus their loyalty from the nation-state to the region.

The European national state is the child of the industrial age. The national states as we know them today were born 200 years ago and have developed in the same rhythm as the industrial society. No wonder then that both the industrial age and the national state reached their climax in the 1960s. Now we see how the industrial society is under attack. It is gradually being crowded out—so to speak— by the immaterial society based on culture, knowledge, and information. The industrial technology (a mechanical technology) is giving way to information technology and biotechnology. With the fading away of the industrial age we see the withering away of the artificial national state.

Opposition to the European Union is to be found among the extreme right (Le Pen, Schönhuber), the old nationalists (Thatcher, old Gaullists), and the extreme left. The broad political center is gradually endorsing the evolution toward a European Union. In fact, we can go so far as to say that no political party can assume governmental responsibility without endorsing the European construction. Mrs. Thatcher fell from power because she did not do that. The RPR in France was in danger of making the same mistake. The Labour Party in Britain has drawn its conclusions and understands that, without endorsing the European construction, it will never be in government again.

We can see how the national states find it more and more difficult to provide the same level of service to their citizens as they did in the heyday of the industrial age. Look back at the 1960s. Remember the public services offered free of charge to the citizens and compare it with the situation today. That tells one more than anything else about the problems of the national state. These difficulties are not a result of an explicit political decision; it has been forced upon politicians in the national states by powers beyond their control. The national states no longer possess the financial and human resources to provide the same kind of services as they did ten, twenty, thirty years ago.

In these circumstances, the artificial national state is struggling to preserve some of its powers to find out which kind of services it should provide and how to finance them. It is extremely difficult for the national state to do so because of the interaction of two strong currents: (1) the combination of economic internationalization and cultural decentralization and (2) the replacement of the industrial society with the immaterial society. These two currents are imposing a totally new concept on the political, economic, social, and cultural structure of Europe.

What happens in a society when individuals feel that economic security, social security, and cultural security are no longer the exclusive competence of the national state? To examine this question, let us first look at Japan in 1945. At that time, the Japanese national state was completely gone—the emperor, the army, and the government. The Japanese transferred their identity from the national state to their enterprises. They transferred the virtues that had made Japan such a strong military power to the industrial sector pointing toward economic and industrial growth.

Europe in 1994 is not Japan in 1945, but there is a similarity. The national state in Europe is under attack, and the European citizens are reacting in the same way the Japanese citizens did in 1945. They are transferring their identity to their enterprises and, to a certain extent, to the trade unions. This goes for economic security, social security, and cultural security.

THE ENTERPRISES AND TRADE UNIONS

This explains the entry into the arena by the fourth main actor—the enterprises and trade unions. The enterprises take over from the national state by offering security and the prospect of cultural identity to the citizens.

Economic security comes first. People today are ready to accept part-time work or a reduction in their wages if that is necessary to keep the enterprise functioning. That is not because the workers want to boost the profits of the firm; they realize that, if they do lose their jobs, the national state cannot offer them others.

Social security comes next. Many people link their pensions to wage fixing and to the existence of the firm. That relationship would not have been considered in the 1960s because, as with economic security, the national state cannot provide pensions in sufficient scale. People must rely on the enterprises.

The enterprises currently provide a chain of social security measures hitherto covered by the national state: supplementary training, reeducation, leisure activities not only for the staff but also for the family of the staff, retirement schemes and ideas for leisure activities for retired people, and school facilities for the children of the staff. This is not the beginning of the end, it is the start of a new beginning.

The national state is not trying to prevent this development from taking place. On the contrary, it is stimulating it. The reason is quite simple. The national state no longer possesses the economic and financial means necessary to maintain the same high standard of social welfare. It looks to the enterprise to step in to relieve it of some of the burden. By doing so it actually invites the enterprise to take over many tasks hitherto under the aegis of the national state.

Cultural security comes third. The national state has never been able to offer a culture. We do not have the Federal Republic of Germany culture, the Great Britain culture, or the Republic of France culture. What we do have is a German or rather German-speaking culture, an English-speaking culture, and a French-speaking culture. With the national state further on the retreat, people find it difficult to see a fixed star for their identity. To a certain extent, they find it in the basic culture, but they also supplement it with a cultural link—an adoption of a set of values—provided by the firm.

A longer and deeper look into cultural security brings into the open two topics of vital importance to the 1990s: the decline of traditional values and the role of the audiovisual media.

The traditional moral values in society are losing strength. Many people think that failure to pay their taxes is not a major offense in the moral sense, although it may be in a legal sense. The borderlines for moral behavior—what is permissible toward one's fellow man and what is not—are constantly being weakened. More and more is permissible. The crimes and semi-crimes that are committed in the wake of these less stringent moral values are jeopardizing the fabric of our societies. One of the results can be seen in our political system. Because moral values are no longer functioning as an unseen part of legislation, the laws must be more and more detailed. Consequently, they become too complicated for the average citizen. The mental distances between the political system and the average citizen are increasing.

It seems that the modern, complex, sophisticated society finds it difficult to work solely on the basis of legal texts because the texts are too difficult to read and understand. This is the background for the appearance of the many people who earn their living by interpreting the law and suing each other. The moral values in society must be in conformity not only with the letter but also the spirit of the law. That is difficult for several reasons. One reason is that laws are often changed. The need for congruity between the letter and the spirit of the law calls for long-lasting laws that impose the spirit and the idea of the law on society and its individuals. Another reason is that law texts are not always clear. A third one is that the lawmakers have not always made up their minds completely to define the objective. A society can work only if there is an unwritten and often unspoken common interpretation of what is permissible and what is not. Legal texts form the framework for that interpretation. In today's society both the framework and the interpretation are under attack.

The enterprises must mobilize the workers and the staff to make sure that there is a common understanding of what is permissible inside the enterprise and what is not. This goes not only for the work time, but also for leisure as the enterprises build themselves up to the role of a cultural factor. As enterprises replace the national state in many respects, including social welfare, the behavior of the workers and the staff outside working hours is no longer irrelevant.

The second topic of vital importance is the role of the audiovisual media. Television is playing an important role in the slide away from firm values to a more fluid interpretation, where some people may regard something as permissible while other people may regard it as highly offensive. Television creates its own reality because the real world is not regarded as being sufficiently interesting, exciting, and sexy to attract viewers. The competition among channels and corporations to get a high number of viewers is sharp, very sharp indeed. If what happens in the real world is not good enough, modern technology makes it possible for the media to create something else to replace the boring reality. In other words, often entertainment takes over from reality but when it is presented to viewers it is nonetheless based on reality. The implication of this is that the viewers (the public) gradually, but with a high degree of certainty, lose their instinct for what is reality and what is imagination or entertainment.

Imagination and entertainment are much more fun. The public does not need to think much or to reflect much. There is no need to take a position, and there is no call for responsibility. The eyes tell the viewer what he or she sees and that is fine. Emotions replace reason as the controlling factor.

The question remains whether this tendency to replace reality with entertainment (or even worse to blur the difference) will continue and if so what the longer term implications for society will be. It is certainly one of the factors behind the delinking of moral values from the legal texts. As the distinction between reality and imagination is blurred so is the idea of what is permissible and what is not permissible.

The problem with the audiovisual media is that they undermine solid information. People want entertainment, not information. Media providing information do so at the risk of being turned off. The entertainment channel is the winner. It does not really matter whether it is genuine or artificial. Technology makes it possible to blur the difference between these two worlds. That may lead to societies where people are bored by information and prefer entertainment and eventually isolate themselves from the real world. Why bother with grievous news about the economy or the crime rate when it is possible to escape by switching to another channel to see Walt Disney present the sexless but happy society, where the good guy always wins. Why bother with the problem of malnutrition when one can enter the painless world by switching to virtual reality.

In Chapter 2 we saw two kinds of seclusion: scientific and national seclusion. Both born in the industrial age, both are fading away with the end of the industrial society. So far so good. If we are not careful, however, the vehicle for this opening and broadening of our minds may produce another, just as dangerous, seclusion: seclusion from reality.

5

The Immaterial Society in Europe

The economic and cultural frontiers of the immaterial society in Europe will follow traditional borders drawn by language and religion, that is, the basic culture. It will, broadly speaking, encompass Western Europe (including the Iberian Peninsula and the British Isles), Northern Europe (including Scandinavia), Central and Eastern Europe close to the frontiers of the German Order in the medieval period (the Baltic States), and the Hapsburg empire vis-à-vis czarist Russia and the Ottoman empire (Poland, the Czech Republic, the Slovak Republic, Hungary, maybe some part of Romania, and about half of Yugoslavia).[1]

The geographical areas outside this line will not be excluded from European development, but it is very unlikely that they will form part of the European Union that finally emerges from this melting pot. Undoubtedly, strong ties will be developed with Russia, which in one form or another will be associated with the European construction; the key word here is ties, not full membership. Russia has always sought to emulate Western Europe, but it has never been successful. The challenge for the European Union, as well as for Russia, is to work out a stable relationship without which the whole European construction will be like a first-rate ship of the line without a mainmast.

We already have an indication of the economic and industrial structure of this Europe. It will be built around a strong and viable center supported by some regional centers. Traditional industries will not weigh heavily. Instead Europe may well be characterized by the science, or rather the art, of human resource development so vital to the two pillars of tomorrow's economic and industrial life: information technology and biotechnology.

The pivot for Europe's economic and technological development is to be found in the broad band around the Rhine, from Amsterdam in the north, encompassing big chunks of Nordrhein-Westfalen, Rheinland-Pfalz, Bayern, Baden-Württemberg, Switzerland, Lombardy, eastern France including Burgundy, the Rhone Valley, the Côte d'Azur, Languedoc, and Catalonia. Only some of these areas exist on the European political and economic maps of today, but they do nonetheless represent genuine regions ready to fulfill a new role not very far from the role they played several hundred years ago. This center will rival strong centers in the United States, the northeastern megalopolis and Los Angeles–San Diego–San Francisco, and Japan. Note that one and a half of these centers is based on the Anglo-Saxon culture; the other half is based upon a Latin American (not Spanish, but Spanish speaking) culture. There are two Japanese centers (Tokyo and Osaka), and new centers in China are building up around Shanghai and Guangzhou–Hong Kong. Europe will be a serious contender in the big international game only if there is at least one such strong center. The existing center is, however, not without its weaknesses. One of them is that it is build around the production of investment machinery which has been but will not necessarily continue to be a growth sector.

The southeastern part of England around London has a strong claim for a role as a supporting regional center. Financial services and intellectual production will pull this regional center ahead. It will never rise to challenge the real center, but its role as a regional center is firmly established for the foreseeable future.

The Iberian Peninsula has several good reasons to claim a role as a regional center: cheap labor, excellent geographical position, and tourism, as well as the multibillion-dollar business of the future—retirement villages for elderly people from various parts of Europe with less temperate weather conditions.

A third regional center may be Vienna-Budapest-Prague—a revival of the Hapsburg empire or rather the old Austria-Hungary. Vienna would be the financial and administrative center, Budapest would be the economic center for a strong agriculturally dominated Hungarian economy, and Prague is situated in the middle of industrial Bohemia. Today, Hungary, the Czech Republic, and the Slovak Republic are ready to take their places in the new Europe.

A fourth center is coming together in the northeastern part of Europe: Denmark, northeastern Germany, northern Poland, the Baltic States, and the south of Sweden. Although some will say this is a revival of the Hanseatic League, there are several differences. This center will not be based on trade but on agriculture, food processing, light industry, energy, environmental protection, transportation, and telecommunications. It is more than likely that the center will be Copenhagen, which is the only city in this part of Europe that can claim to be both a Nordic and a European capital and is the only city that offers all the facilities (transportation, communications, culture, leisure, good environment) needed by a city acting as a pivot. Amazingly enough, very few people have grasped that the unification of Germany, the political and economic liberalization going on in Poland and the Baltic States, and Sweden's determination to enter the European Union will change the status of Copenhagen from a picturesque, medium-sized capital to one of the most promising geographical locations in the European economic theater for decades to come.

European business seems to adapt well to these new circumstances—at least as well as their American and Japanese competitors. For a long time, the industrial dinosaurs have been dead and buried, almost alive. They could not keep pace with the development and suffered the same agonizing process as their real ancestors many million years ago.

European business seems to be thriving, or at least starting to thrive, in the era of competition where the hitherto relatively simple selection of costs has been replaced by a panoply of parameters such as technology, total product, design, quality, service, and environment. To fix the appropriate mix of these parameters in a given market at a given time is quite simply what strategy is all about. It can be done only by having access to financial resources and human resources. Thus the whole strategy is, in fact, simple enough to carry out but quite difficult to implement.

The Europeans will be in an advantageous position because the new era, which emphasizes design, service, and technology, disengages itself from physical production. It is not a question of producing something efficiently at a low cost. It is a question of finding out what to produce on the basis of long-term consumer preferences. A different skill is required compared not only to the industrial society, based on industrial culture and industrial technology, but also to the postindustrial society, based on information technology and biotechnology wrapped into the structure of the old industrial society.

Now we are truly entering a new frontier—a new age of mankind which may be termed The Immaterial Society. One of the implications in this new society is the struggle for supremacy with regard to values, norms, attitudes—in short, culture. Another implication is the complete change of business life. The industrial enterprise is already dead. The diversified producer of ideas is in. To achieve success, one needs an input of many different, often contradictory, ideas that can be amalgamated into one, single concept. This requires access to many different cultures and subcultures. This competition is in regard to ideas, which is why the big monoliths are breaking up and why decentralization inside the firm is coming into vogue. Obviously, networks in one way or another are much better than fusions. It is of paramount importance to preserve and safeguard different corporate cultures when several firms enter into cooperation or an outright merger. Sometimes it may even serve the purpose of the firm to encourage subcultures inside the firm to stimulate cultural competition. The situation is parallel to economic competition. A competitive surrounding is a prerequisite for staying on top of the world. The European cultural mosaic provides a much better starting position for this race than the mix of cultures found in Japan or the United States.

The challenge for the European Union is to resist the temptation to centralize power. The Soviet empire fell apart because of centralization. This error of judgment must not be repeated by the European Union. Fortunately, the Europeans seem to have learned the lesson. Contrary to many people's beliefs, the European Union is moving not toward centralization but toward decentralization. There is no doubt that the economic and monetary union will be decentralized in the same way as the Federal Reserve System and the German Bundesbank. The implementation of the single market is not being performed by the union itself but is being left to existing institutions (European standardization institutions). A fundamental principle in the negotiations concerning a political union is decentralization (subsidiarity). But many people still see the union with glasses more than twenty years old when the keyword was total harmonization. Fortunately, that was twenty years ago! The European construction can succeed only if minorities, their languages, and their religions are protected in the forthcoming treaties.

The European model is not so distant from the statecraft that kept the Hapsburg empire going for centuries under extremely difficult conditions. The Hapsburgs succeeded in welding together a state by striking the right balance between centralized and decentralized power. Oddly enough their dividing line was very similar to the one mentioned above. Every time they tried to centralize more, one or more of the people (nationalities) threatened to break out; every time the reins became too loose, the state threatened to cease to exist. Such tightrope walking is called for once again. Another example is present-day Switzerland. To all those, and there are many, who say that it is not possible to have a state with many languages, the appropriate answer is to look at the Hapsburg empire and Switzerland. But do not forget to add that it will work only with the right distribution of power between the center and the regions.

The strong, and necessary, glue for this process to succeed is culture and an esprit de corps emanating from the European enterprises. Businesses will no longer be only economic operators but will come to take an active part in the whole process of offering and providing economic, social, and cultural security to all Europeans. Not only will enterprises have a more important role to play as a kind of replacement for the national state, on the macro-level, but also will have much more influence vis-à-vis the local communities on the micro-level.

Many local communities have given up fruitless attempts to gain support from the national state for social and cultural policies. They now embrace the enterprises that offer to provide exactly such support. We see a new symbiosis: Local communities attract enterprises, and enterprises support the economic, social, and cultural life of the local community they have chosen.

The coming of the immaterial society and the increased importance of human capital explain why so many economic policy prognoses have gone wrong during the last decade. The behaviors of enterprises and people do not follow the same pattern as they did in the industrial age. Market forces are different. The introduction of product concept completely changes the demand structure. Human capital requires a kind of investment totally different than that of plants and machinery.

NOTE

1. This is, of course, not without exception. Greece for example has been a member of the European Community since 1981. Romania and Bulgaria are also moving toward the European Union.

6

Europe, the United States, and the Far East: The Next Ten Years

1994 TO 2004

If one could look back on the decade from 1994 to 2004 from the future, one would be able to understand from these examples the difficulties faced by futurists. Nearly all the prognoses made in the beginning of the 1990s were proven wrong. Too cautious, they underestimated the evolution and changes that would take place. They did not sufficiently integrate internationalization, technological development, and the emergence of new set of values. Even if the preceding quarter of a century had given ample proof of accelerating development this was not fully grasped in 1994. There were three main reasons behind these appallingly poor prognoses.

First, very few people perceived that, around 1990, the world changed from continuous to discontinuous evolution. The world made a qualitative jump. Experience indicates that the prognoses tend to be wrong exactly when evolution changes track from continuity to discontinuity.

Second, interdisciplinary and intercultural perspectives made their impact with incredible power during the 1990s. Mankind moved away from the singular approach, specialization, and the outlook of overspecialized persons toward imagination—even fantasy—combination, supervision, and teamwork.

Third, the world moved from a decade of technology in the 1970s, through the decade of economy in the 1980s, toward a decade of culture, values, and human resources in the 1990s. At last, the shackles put in place by industrial technology were cast away. Formerly, in the age of mechanical engineering, we could measure everything in square meters, cubic meters, tons, horsepower, and so on. When we moved into the immaterial society, it became clear that most human activity could no longer be measured in such concrete terms.

One of the great turning points in history occurred in the beginning of the 1990s. For several hundred years, particularly after the French revolution and during the beginning of the industrial age, we have lived in the era of the Anglo-Saxon culture. First the British, in the colonial days, and then the Americans spread this culture around the world. It has been universally recognized as *the* culture. That is no longer the case. The Anglo-Saxon culture, as well as its apparent monopoly of ideas and norms, is being questioned more every day. That does not mean that another culture has taken over, but it does mean that the culture's monopoly and its universal respect, not to say obedience, have vanished. This is indeed a watershed, even if it is not yet clear.

The literature has recently given birth to an increasing number of books contesting the conventional wisdom that the Anglo-Saxon culture was a blessing to the non–Anglo-Saxon populations brought under the control of this culture on new continents. In the United States, many of the forgotten cultures of small peoples have reappeared. Many of the rituals of these cultures and many of their beliefs, brushed aside by the strong and conquering Anglo-Saxon culture, have reentered the arena. More significant, many of the atrocities committed by the standard-bearers of this culture are now being questioned after decades and even centuries of silence. It was common knowledge, until one or two decades ago, that the United States was created by the Anglo-Saxon culture as a magnanimous and humane culture softly guiding other cultures and the peoples attached to them. That is no longer so. History must be rewritten. The actions committed by the Anglo-Saxon culture are now being described as what they always were—acts of great brutality committed to destroy other cultures and other peoples. The flywheel of this observation is that it is happening now after long periods during which nobody dared or cared to write about it. They do now. Let us not forget one simple thing: History is written and told by the winners, not by the losers. The fact that the truth is coming out now is a strong indication that the Anglo-Saxon culture is no longer a winner.

This revolt against one dominating culture—Anglo-Saxon culture—appears, among other things, in movements organized around indigenous people. There are nearly 250 million indigenous people around the world. Two million Inuits in the Arctic area are found in the national states of Canada, Denmark, and Russia. In America, 42 million Indians, with such proud names as Mohawks, Yanomanis, Amarakaeris, Quiches, and Shuars, are found. In Africa and the Middle East are 25 million, including Bedouins, Dinkas, Masais, Efes, and Sans. In Southeast Asia 32 million include Hmongs, Karens, Penans, Hanunoos, and Danis. In South Asia, there are 74 million, among them Gonds, Bhils, Santhais, Chakmas, and Veddas. In Oceania there are 3 million Aborigines, Maoris, and Kanaks. In the northeastern part of Asia there are 85 million, most of whom are Bulans, Ainus, and Uighurs. These names are not exclusive but constitute the most numerous tribes of indigenous peoples.

Until recently these people lived a quiet life without publicly voicing their origins. Many of them would probably rather have forgotten that they came from an indigenous people and did not fall into one of the large groups of industrialized people. They are no longer hiding below the surface. They feel that the time has come to appear in the open and claim their rights. Once again, we meet a clear and unmistaken sign that a cultural turbulence is taking place.

The English language is the universal language, but not because it represents the English or the American culture. It is the universal language because it is the computer language. English has become a language without a basic culture exactly as Latin became, during a large part of the Middle Ages, an instrument of communication.

The herald of all this came on to the stage in 1989—the bicentenary for the great French revolution—with the revolution in Central and Eastern Europe. This liberation of the minds of people hitherto suppressed by an evil ideology started the process. It made it clear that mankind now faced a qualitative leap. The forces that triggered the revolution in Central and Eastern Europe are analogous to the forces behind the great French revolution in 1789: a suppression of free speech by a small, self-appointed elite with the large majority as victims and an economic system which, in the end, barely managed to feed the population.

Astonishingly enough, the clash between the apparently incompatible topics of economic internationalization in Western Europe and cultural decentralization in Central and Eastern Europe is being amalgamated into a European model of society in the decade from the beginning of the 1990s to the beginning of the next century—the 21st century. Internationalization takes over with regard to economies, monetary questions, industry, and technology. Decentralization (regions and local communities) takes over with regard to cultural and social questions and education.

This is hardly as surprising as a futuristic prediction of this kind would have been ten years ago. In the historical periods during which Europe has approached some kind of unity, the right balance has always been found between items to be left to nationalities and peoples on a decentralized level.

In a way, the idea of Europe consists and has always consisted of various subcultures competing among themselves to shape the European civilization. What is happening in the 1990s is new for our generation, but it is in fact a repetition of fundamental ties in the history of European civilization. They made themselves known in a spectacular way every time European civilization went through a phase of discontinuity toward a quality jump.

THE POWER GAME

The decisive factor in the international power game in the 1990s is the diminishing importance of military power and the increasing importance of culture, communication, and a set of values, ethics, and ideas as the spearhead in the struggle for power and influence. The industrial society and the industrial technology gave birth to big military machines which were used from the Napoleonic wars until after World War II. The objective of these earlier wars was to win a military battle over enemy armies, but gradually another objective made its entrance: the destruction of the industrial potential of the opponent. To achieve this objective, it was not sufficient to destroy the military forces of the enemy; it became necessary to transform factories, supply lines, and the infrastructure into a heap of rubble. The big bombardments of Germany and Japan are cases in point. This way to approach things is fully in conformity with the love of the industrial society for what is big, harmonized, and massive.

When the balance of power changed at the end of the 1980s, it became clear that the Soviet military threat had been overestimated, and, at the same time, the U.S. military power began to attract considerable attention. It was brought into action with success in the beginning of 1991 with Operation Desert Storm. It was the last war in which the war machine of the industrial age was in action. It was the first war in which the command of the electromagnetic spectrum was decisive (the so-called C3I: control, communication, command, and intelligence). During the 1990s the U.S. military will undergo a complete restructuring. The big army units equipped to fight a conventional armored battle will be replaced by mobile units. Big sums of money will be used to construct a limited edition of SDI to protect the United States against—not a full-scale strategic attack—but a limited missile attack from abroad; let us call it missile terrorism. In the same mold fall the training and equipment of special units to combat international terrorism. The U.S. military doctrine will gradually be dominated by ideas to search out terrorism anywhere in the world while at the same time trying to protect the United States against missiles in possession of terrorists or states giving refuge to terrorists. This turnaround in the structure of the U.S. military superpower implies a good-bye to a grand-scale conventional military machine.

Several factors explain this development. The most important one is that not even the United States can afford to support the military machine of earlier decades. The development and production of weapon systems have become so expensive that only a limited number can actually be purchased. Military strategy and military tactics will undergo consistent change because this very costly, almost irreplaceable, equipment cannot be used. It is simply too expensive to replace. War on a big scale has become a thing of the past. The threat of war is diminishing. Bullying and deterrence become aces in military strategy. There is a clear parallel here to the medieval period when princes could afford costly armies of mercenaries but could not afford to risk them in battle. At that time, military tactics consisted mainly of complicated maneuvers designed to put the enemy in an untenable position which inevitably opened the way for peace negotiations. The most adroit maneuver (not actual battle) earned the upper hand. There is also a clear analogy in World War I to dreadnought terror with the concept of fleet in being. The new thing here is that this kind of maneuver is changing from the actual battlefield to the technological level. The question is not whether one can outfight the enemy but whether one can outcommunicate the enemy. If one can succeed in outcommunicating the enemy, the enemy will not dare wage an actual war.

In contrast to this diminishing warfare, economic war—economic competition—becomes more tense. The economic war will take on dimensions that were unthinkable during the 1980s. Many military strategies will be adopted by leaders in economic and industrial life. During the 1990s the world will watch with astonishment the power games between the big multinational companies. These power games will be more violent and irascible than ever before. Some of the well-known multinational giants will be destroyed. Others will surrender and continue to exist on a lower level on the economic and technological ladder. They will have to transfer certain products, certain projects, and certain national markets just as the losing national state in 19th-century wars had to cede certain geographical areas.

As the decade progresses, it will become clear that the national states do not have much influence on the economic wars between the big multinational companies. One of the consequences of economic internationalization is that the big enterprises spread their activities among various national states. This makes it extremely difficult for a national state to define its interest in such an economic war. Typically, it will be associated in one way or another with both combatants. This state of affairs will be one of the main reasons that individual human beings will transfer their identity from the national state to the enterprises.

Power is the ability to make someone do something other than what he or she originally intended to do. Three instruments can be used to impose one's will on someone else: military power, financial transfers, and persuasion (culture). During the 1990s, culture, knowledge, and information will take over from military power and financial transfers as a decisive instrument for exercising power. It is in conformity with the phasing out of the industrial society and the phasing in of information technology. Military power cannot be used unless one has perfect control of information. The economic competition cannot be won without the same control. Knowledge and information become the primary competitive parameters. Cultural decentralization enhances this evolution. Every individual becomes more and more conscious about which set of values determines what is good and what is wrong.

With the phasing out of the industrial society, plants, and machinery, the individual and human resources come into focus. After 200 years, during which the machine dominated the individual, it starts all over again. Individuals will enter the stage with the justified demand to exploit all their potential.

In a historical perspective, power politics since 1945 have been atypical. We have been living in a bipolar world with two challengers—the United States and the Soviet Union—offering different societies and collecting client states under their political, military, economic, and cultural umbrellas. To a very large extent, we have witnessed an ideological competition, in which the two systems have presented themselves as alternatives and have imposed upon the other states the need to choose. Such an ideological competition is very rare in the history of mankind, and it can without any hesitation be classified as a parenthesis between periods dominated by a more normal international power game.

With the decline and fall of the Soviet Union, this bipolar world disappeared from the stage. Some observers take the position that the new order will be a tripolar world with three regional blocks: the United States–North America, Japan–East Asia, and EEC–Europe. To be fair, that was how it looked in the beginning of the 1990s, but gradually something very different will appear. Before we embark into that, however, it is important to analyze the traditional structure of power politics in an international context. We have three key words: the center, the hinterland, and the periphery.

The center is the leader with regard to ideas and values (culture) and is in possession of the military and financial resources required to get its own way. Until the end of World War I the center rotated among various countries and regions in Europe. After World War I it moved to the United States. Until the 1960s it was firmly anchored in the northeastern part of the United States around the axis New York–Boston, but from the middle of the 1960s it began to move westward toward California where a new breakthrough with regard to culture, ideas, and values was made; for example, protection of the environment, leisure, and the audiovisual culture based on Hollywood's endless production of pictures and idols.

The crucial point in the definition of the center is that it attracts talents from the outside. It works as a magnet in the interplay between technology and culture shaping the fabric of society. The center is the self-evident, indeed the only, place where the cultural and technological elite has the resources and intellectual fortitude to make the breakthroughs without which civilization cannot exist. In addition, a genuine center must possess military power and financial means. The combination of military power and financial control over the rest of the world and fusion of a cultural and technological elite dwarfs any challenger.

The role of the hinterland is to support the center by placing auxiliary troops at the disposal of the center, accepting financial transfers into the center, and allowing the cultural and technological elite to move to the center. This far from glorious role is to support the center and to contribute to the power of the center and possibly the application of power by the center. The reward is that the center directly or indirectly guarantees its military security, its economic stability and growth, and a certain but not excessive share of the ideas produced by the cultural and technological elite.

We speak here about a patron-client relationship. At the very moment the center is no longer capable of rewarding the hinterland, there is no reason for the hinterland to stay attached to the center. It will try to establish itself as a challenger. The partnership works only as long as both partners profit.

When the center moved from Europe to the United States, Europe had to accept the role as hinterland for the new center. This role was never seriously contested until about 1990 when a new, confident Europe began to question its role as support for the center, the United States. Exactly the same thing happened in Japan which, until around 1990, was content to be hinterland for the United States but then began to question the continuation of this role.

What happened around 1990 was that the two hinterlands for the American center raised the question whether the United States was sufficiently strong militarily, economically, technologically, and culturally to continue as the uncontested center. This question will dominate international politics during most of the 1990s.

The role of the periphery is even less enviable. It delivers raw material to the center and, to a certain degree, also to the hinterland. It buys what is produced in the center and hinterland, although it is frequently of second-rate quality. It is not supposed to ask questions. Before World War I the colonies of the European empires constituted the classic example. After World War II the former colonies got their independence but were kept in the role as periphery. It was their desire to change this situation that explains the demand for a new economic world order, and it was also this situation that led to a number of limited wars including Iraq's unsuccessful attempt to annex Kuwait. During the 1990s, the developing nations will continue to try to emancipate themselves from the role as periphery, but they will not succeed, because they lack the military power, the economic strength and technology, and the culture to force such a change upon the United States, Europe, and Japan.

The 1990s will bring out into the open that the great game is moving away from the bipolar world (the United States and the Soviet Union) toward the reestablishment of the well-known, well-tried power structure based upon center, hinterland, and periphery.

THE UNITED STATES: THE MILITARY VECTOR

After the fall of the Soviet empire, that is from around 1990, the United States had complete supremacy in the military area. However, the picture is different with regard to economy, technology, and culture.

The United States has a firm grip on one of the three vectors of power: military power. But it is not easy to apply military power without economic and financial strength and a firm cultural basis. How is it possible to apply military power if one cannot pay for it? Why is military power needed when one questions the basic values in one's own society? These two questions, fundamental around 1990, still seem to be unanswered. For a large part of the 1990s, the United States will try to keep in rein its allies inside existing military alliances and accordingly under American dominance through the military vector. It will become, however, more and more difficult because the former common enemy, the Soviet Union, has disappeared from sight. The United States will not know, literally speaking, what to use its big military machine for. Doubts will be enhanced during the decade as it becomes clear that military power is a kind of paper tiger which cannot compete effectively with the economic strength of East Asia and the new cultural enlightenment in Europe.

An X-ray made in the beginning of the 1990s showed a strong United States with regard to economy, industry, and culture. But an X-ray is a static analysis. It shows how things are, not in which direction they are moving. If we look instead at tendencies, it is clear that the United States is on a downward slope. The American economy is not strong. American competitiveness is unable to keep pace with Japan and Europe. The United States is still the world power in the area of new technology, but not to the extent it was during earlier decades. Not very much indicates that the United States will be able to turn around this rather dismal picture during the 1990s. We may see interruptions, but probably not a reversal, of the basic tendency. It is a striking blow to realize that the

United States, which formerly had promoted free trade, in 1990 started to flirt with protectionist tendencies.

Two significant tendencies explain the problems facing the United States during the coming decade. First, as the United States withdraws from its engagement around the globe, it will become more occupied by its own problems and its own interests in the Western Hemisphere. The free trade agreement with Mexico and Canada will pave the way for an economic and commercial arrangement encompassing the whole of the Western Hemisphere. Ten years from now, the United States will still be the strongest power in the world, but already in the beginning of the 1990s the United States has ceased to be the all-dominating superpower ready and capable of defending its global interests. The posture adopted by the United States vis-à-vis the former Yugoslavia is a case in point. The United States has backed away from sending troops to that area. Although there may be several reasons, one of them undoubtedly is that the United States no longer automatically takes on a global responsibility.

Second, the American society has become engulfed in internal confrontations and increasing doubts about the hitherto uncontested American model. What gave the United States its strength in 1950 was the phenomenal belief in "the American way of life." The Americans themselves believed in that model. All other nations found it attractive and tried to emulate it. It gave a moral strength comparable to that of imperial Britain a century earlier as explained by Kipling ("The burden of the white man"). By 1990 many Americans had lost faith in their nation and their society. Nothing is more dangerous. This is both an omen and a contributing factor to the decline of the hitherto uncontested power position of the Anglo-Saxon culture.

These two factors explain the perplexity that is emanating from the United States during the 1990s. The arrival of several new cultures, able to launch and defend a new set of values and put cultural competition on the agenda, is one of the encouraging signs.

EAST ASIA: THE FINANCIAL AND TECHNOLOGICAL VECTOR

East Asia's claim to assume the role of the center is to be found in the sphere of technology. The 1990s will see an incredible, even fantastic, stream of new projects developed, produced, and marketed in East Asia. The world may gasp when faced with this stream of new technology. Once and for all we leave the technology of the industrial age, the technology of power, and enter into the era of information technology (the technology of collecting, channeling, and transforming knowledge). More than 25 percent of the gross national product channeled to investment in conjunction with a well-defined industrial and technological policy will enable East Asia to take the lead looking back to measure its distance from the United States and Europe. Japan is supported by and, in turn, supports a whole string of small states (Singapore, Taiwan, Hong Kong, Korea, Thailand, and later in the decade Vietnam). These states are all able to change gears from a lower technology to a higher technology. Education is a key to every success. In general terms, they manage to put human resources before development of plants and machinery. The contrast to the United States is very stark indeed. Ten years from now, Eastern Asia will be the world's uncontested economic and technological power center after a ten-year period of phenomenal growth.

In a military context, the region will not succeed in shaping its own policy. The American withdrawal from military bases will create an unmanageable insecurity. It is defined by an aversion throughout the Far East to the idea of Japan in a military role. If various circumstances develop unfavorably, military conflicts may destabilize the region and blow the economic miracle to pieces with a big bang. There is a clear risk in the northwestern Pacific where the spheres of interest of the United States, Japan, Russia, and China collide. Such a collision of the spheres of interest of various powerful states has been seen before in the history of mankind. Often it has given rise to military conflicts. The second big risk is to be found in the Indian Ocean. The encapsulation of India by Arab Islamic countries and the world's most populous Islamic country (Indonesia) does not lend itself to a very stable situation.

The decisive factor in Asia has been and is whether Japan can exercise leadership. It is not certain that the Japanese strength with regard to finance and technology can be translated into political leadership. Japan managed before the 1990s because it had a homogeneous society, a set of values sponsoring economic expansion, and many other factors, not the least of which was the ability to miniaturize, which, in the age of information technology and biotechnology, became one of vital importance.

The Japanese society was homogeneous—ideologically and socially. The Japanese were firm in their conviction that they were selected by God with the duty and the right to lead, not to say dominate, other peoples and other nations. The individual found his or her identity as a member of the group and was unsure how to behave as an individual. Obligations and advantages followed from adherence to a group. The decisive point was the interest of the group, not the right of the individual. The striving for consensus, a characteristic of Japanese society, follows from this particular aspect of society. Decisions were taken not by the persons involved, but by the group. Responsibility became blurred, and decision-making procedures became obscure and impenetrable to the outside world.

To the outside world, Japan appeared to be one group with unanimity among all its subgroups and individuals. This was not only a façade, it was a reality. Suffice it to mention that pressure from the United States to raise the value of the yen was duly accommodated, but not without a corresponding increase in productivity which kept competitiveness unchanged. The workers possessed an esprit de corps, a company culture, and they regarded the American pressure as an attack from an outside aggressor that demanded an appropriate defense by the group.

This island mentality is fragile. It creates mistrust and fear toward the outside world. An island mentality is a defensive mentality. It has been a psychological barrier to Japanese engagement in world politics and international economic policy reflecting Japan's technological strength. In fact, it was a brake on the evolution toward an organization of Eastern Asia which craved Japanese leadership, not only politicians but statesmen. It was a paradox. Japan itself needed the surrounding world, but the Japanese fortress mentality blocks the way even as we approach the beginning of the new century. Japan has not succeeded in escaping from its self-imposed prison. The question is whether Japan can do so during the 1990s.

There are other indications of a weakened Japanese society. One of them is the increasing number of old people. Furthermore, the younger generation feels more emancipated from the traditional values of Japanese society. Young people are squeezed between the culture from the outside and the domestic culture. They have not yet managed to find the appropriate answer, but they manage to carry on as if there were no problems.

During his visit to the ASEAN countries in 1992, Japanese Prime Minister Miyazawa launched his doctrine by saying that Japan would never be a military superpower and that Japan would consequently shape its foreign policy by taking into account regional aspects. This doctrine reflects the Japanese attitude toward its neighbors not only in the ASEAN area, but also in the Far East. It shows Japan with a low profile on the military side and, to compensate for that, a beefing up of other aspects of the foreign policy. All of these factors explain why Japan will not be able to put its mark on the cultural pattern in the same way it has on the technological pattern.

China may have a better chance to succeed in this. It requires, however, a delicate handling from both sides—China and the rest of the world. The Chinese outlook has always been that the rest of the world approaches China, not the other way around. Since the Chinese emperor 500 years ago locked maps and travel reports into a safe to prevent Chinese adventurers and discoverers from following in the footsteps of the bold Chinese seafarers who were exploring the Indian Ocean, China has always taken the view that the world can come to China. That perspective has lost its meaning in today's international world. Indeed, one of the hallmarks of modern Chinese politics is that China has begun to understand that it is up to China to enter the world. The problem is that this is uncharted waters for the Chinese mind. The rest of the world must understand that and play the game. That means a mixture of accommodation and conditions. It would be a mistake not to understand that this process can succeed only if certain limits are drawn which cannot be transgressed by China without consequences.

The intriguing question is whether this will lead to the fall of communism in China and whether that will lead to some kind of democracy in the Western mold. We will have to wait some time for those answers. A Westerner might think that this development would favor such an approach, but it is dangerous to judge the evolution of China with Western eyes.

The Chinese culture and Chinese civilization are strong enough to challenge the Anglo-Saxon culture and the emerging European cultural powerhouse, but that can happen only if and when the Chinese themselves move closer to the world and understand the rest of the world better. That includes the question of human rights. Such a movement will undoubtedly take some time.

In the meantime, Europeans and Americans should understand that a very demanding process is occurring. Our reaction to this Chinese development—unprecedented in Chinese history—will be closely monitored. The Chinese, as indeed other Asian peoples, have their own standards for moral, ethical, and human rights. They regard their standards as perfectly legitimate even if they differ from European and American standards.

EUROPE: THE CULTURAL VECTOR

The fear that Europeans might be compelled to adopt a harmonized and common culture is far from reality. On the contrary, Europe's strength in the 1990s is exactly the opposite: a cultural diversification opening the gate for many competing cultures striving to catch the soul of every individual European. Europe will become the place for new ideas and new lifestyles. It can clearly be seen in industrial life where Europe has a strong position in software, biotechnology, and the service sector, including financial services and transport.

Somewhat surprisingly, during the 1990s, the old Europe gradually will come to guide the new culture and the new cultural tendencies. Europe will replace California as the leader deciding which way to go with regard to culture and ideas. That will create an irresistible optimism and self-confidence. The European industrial life will benefit from the new order between culture and economics; that is, culture (ideas and attitudes) creates economic wealth, not the other way around.

THE NEW CENTERS

There are seven big power centers in today's world:

* Along the Rhine and the Rhone valleys, Switzerland, Lombardy, a part of southern France, and northern Spain
* Boston, New York, Philadelphia, and Washington, D.C.
* San Francisco, Los Angeles, and San Diego
* Tokyo-Osaka (one or two centers because of the short distance)
* Hong Kong and Guangzhou
* Shanghai
* Taiwan and the opposite coast of China (Fujian province).

The area around Singapore, which encompasses three nations, is also a strong contender for a place on this list. Other centers may appear as runners-up: Bombay is an example; Mexico and Brazil may produce such centers; in time, perhaps Ho Chi Minh City in Vietnam will be one.

These centers will compete, indeed struggle, with each other to possess influence in the form of knowledge and information (culture) to be the leader, that is the center. This competition is not yet settled. During the next decade or two, one or two of these centers will emerge as a leader. The others will be degraded to hinterland. The outcome will be influenced by the declining importance of the military vector, and the fact that it does not really matter which national state is the home of the centers. Note that three of these centers are transnational.

TRILATERALISM

The world has moved away from the American hegemony to some sort of interim trilateralism based upon the United States, the European Union, and Japan. Trilateralism will continue, but not in the form we know it today.

The United States will try to impose itself as the center in a big economic trade bloc encompassing the whole Western Hemisphere. The free trade agreements with Canada and Mexico are the first step in this direction. The idea of President Bush to include the rest of the Western Hemisphere in this concept is a further step. Combined with the American influence in the Persian Gulf this gives the United States a greater control over primary products in the coming decade. Surprisingly enough, the U.S. economy and the American dollar seem to be on the road to making an impact on the world economy in the sector of primary products instead of high technology. The whole concept of the Western Hemisphere as an economic and trade policy zone is not designed to promote high technology but is of interest mainly to the producers of primary products and more or less old-fashioned manufactured goods. The same goes for the strong U.S. treaties with countries in the Middle East. The links with Australia and New Zealand point in the same direction. The American stance in the Uruguay Round further supports this observation.

For some period of time during the Uruguay Round, the United States pressed for concessions in goods not belonging to the category of high technology. Examples of this can be seen in the demand for the opening of the Japanese rice market and the drive to reduce agricultural support in Europe. These moves are laudable but unexpected from a high-technology country.

Japan will dominate East Asia and a large part of Southeastern Asia by a continuous and irresistible economic, industrial, and technological expansion. Japanese firms are going international in the sense that they are allocating subsidiaries all over the globe. Nowhere is it more striking than in East Asia and Southeastern Asia. The technological powerhouse developing in Japan will overshadow anything ever seen or known in the United States. This new perception of technology and its application are spreading fast to other parts of Asia under the superb control of the strong Japanese enterprises. At the same time, traditional labor-intensive production has a strong foothold in the region and will undoubtedly maintain that position. All indicators are therefore that in the coming decade, East Asia will take over in technology and manufacturing.

The Japanese economy has been recently harassed, however, by a financial crisis. It might even be called a financial crash even if the policy makers in Japan have been clever enough to conceal the magnitude of this crisis. This crisis, however, does not detract from our prognosis. As soon as this crisis has been solved—sometime during 1994 or 1995—the Japanese economy will resume its expansionist path.

The European Union will forge a strong and viable European economy under its aegis. The single market is a pile driver in this process. The flywheel will be the German manufacturing industry with machinery and equipment as the ace in the card game. Europe will not be able to match the United States in what may be termed the future dollar-sphere with regard to primary products, nor will Europe equal East Asia with regard to technology and labor-intensive manufactured goods. Europe's competitive advantage will be concentrated in the service sector and some specific areas in food processing, manufacturing, and high technology.

Central and Eastern Europe will gradually but with great certainty be drawn into this economic sphere. The European EFTA countries are already de facto members albeit without the advantages of formal membership which, hopefully, they will achieve in 1995.

THE INTERNATIONAL TRADE SYSTEM

The 1990s will produce a trade system fundamentally different from the one created almost forty years ago. There will be three main differences.

First, instead of one economic superpower, the world will see three big, powerful economic blocs struggling to assume much needed leadership in economic, monetary, and trade problems. The United States used to be the captain on board this ship, but its weakened economic and technological position has undermined its leadership to the extent that the United States now shies away from this responsibility. Neither Europe nor Japan has the economic clout, the technological know-how, or the political will to take over in the foreseeable future.

Second, the world trade system will not be homogeneous but based upon different principles governing three broad sectors.

The first sector comprises products and goods where the supply exceeds the demand. Obvious candidates are agriculture, to a certain extent processed foodstuffs, perhaps cars, steel, shipbuilding, and textiles. The world will witness a game of musical chairs in which the three blocs will try to pass the buck to each other. In other words, in these sectors, we should not count too much on a liberal trade system. Protectionist attitudes and protectionist policies are likely to be applied. The struggle not to be left with the burden of excess supply will be extremely fierce.

The second sector comprises the rest of the processed foodstuffs and the large part of manufactured goods. It is not likely that protectionist policies will be able to make inroads into a liberal trade system. The internationalization of the firm produces a very strong lobby ready to protect and defend a liberal trade system without which the big multinational firms will not be able to operate. Vested interests turn away from nation-oriented protectionism toward supporting a liberal trade system.

The third sector is the most interesting, but also the most complicated, one. It comprises the service sector. Regrettably it has not been possible to include the service sector in the GATT system with a full application of the MFN-clause. This is somewhat surprising taking into consideration that the service sector will be the pull factor of the world economy in the 1990s.

The Uruguay Round succeeded to some extent in liberalizing trade in the service sectors, but unfortunately it did not go far enough. Some rules were adopted but not to their full extent. We will thus still see the rule of the jungle govern a large part of the service sector in the next ten years. That will unquestionably be a brutal, rough, and costly competitive battle involving firms, nations, and international organizations in a lawless pursuit of extremely strong economic interests. This applies especially to the communications and transportation sectors. What is at stake here is a slice of the most lucrative business of all: the economic and technological activity required to link the world together in the coming information and communications society. The survivors of this battle will be the economic giants of the future.

The negotiations were completely distorted. Looked at from the outside, the main question has been agriculture and the main antagonists have been the United States and Europe. Agriculture is not—far from it—the most important economic sector of the future. What really were at stake during the Uruguay Round were the rules concerning communications and the exchange of information. There is already strong evidence that the large transnational enterprises are buying rights to be carriers of information on various national markets. This behavior does not reflect rational economic decisions. It is promoted by the fear that a failure of the Uruguay Round will lead to national barriers against transnational or foreign enterprises specializing in the transmission of information. To protect themselves against such an occurrence, the transnational enterprises are establishing themselves on each of the most important national markets.

Some years ago, the French firm Alcatel, primarily a producer of communications equipment, purchased rights as a carrier of information on the U.S. market. British Telecom has established links with an American enterprise (MCI) to the same effect. French (France Telecom) and German (Deutsche Bundespost Telekom) telecoms are linking up, they have formed a partnership with Sprint (the third largest American long distance operator). Alcatel seems to be interested in linking up with France Telecom thereby positioning itself as a carrier on the European level.

It should be noted that no geographical location can dream about a competitive advantage if it is not linked to the international communications network and the transportation systems. Without these assets, all other advantages, whatever they are, become of no value. With these assets, the race is not won, far from it, but the geographical location in question has ensured itself a place in the race. In the industrial age, a hub was a city or place well positioned to take advantage of transport— railways, shipping, and air transport. That is still a good card to possess, but it must be supplemented by access to another transportation net, the transportation of information and knowledge. Tomorrow's hubs will be chosen from among those places that offer the best information channels at the lowest prices. A hub in the traditional sense, but one without smooth and cost-effective access to the international communications network, is no hub at all but a forgotten and overlooked place.

The strategy of Singapore is revealing. Until recently, Singapore was a transportation hub with regard to shipping and air transport. Now the government of Singapore has launched an attempt to place Singapore on the world map as a hub in the communications age.

After the completion of the Uruguay Round, some conclusions can be drawn and some forecasting is not to be disregarded.

The Uruguay Round was primarily a draw between the industrialized countries and the immaterial societies. Most of the results in terms of liberalization are to be found in the industrial sector (tariff reductions). This points to a slight advantage for the industrialized countries when weighing the benefits for different countries and groups of countries. The pertinent observation is that the industrial countries are not necessarily the United States, Western Europe, and Japan. The most industrialized countries in today's world are to be found outside this triangle. They are to be found, instead, in the Far East, some areas of Southern Asia, and some areas of Latin America. In fact, some of the countries in the Far East received a significant advantage out of the result even if they did not participate in the toughest part of the negotiation. This bears out the statement that the trade rules are written by the largest trading partner. Europe and the United States are still the largest trading partners, but the emerging influence of the Far East as an industrial exporter was clearly felt. The Asian economies will gain most from a result composed of market openings for industrial goods, but not very much with regard to the service sectors where they are not yet fully competitive. The reductions in the support to agriculture can, by the way, be used as a pretext by some Asian governments to implement a policy they wanted for decades.

The coming immaterial societies did not succeed in securing market access for the services they had hoped for. They will come to regret that, but they can blame only themselves. The Europeans allowed the Americans to distort the negotiations by concentrating on agriculture instead of on the service sector. Indeed, that is what the Americans wanted when the negotiations started in the mid-1980s, but midway, about 1990, they were drawn away from that objective. Only a concerted European-American drive to secure a breakthrough could have ensured an opening of the markets for the service sector. Unfortunately, it did not happen.

In the final phase of the negotiations, the Americans did press very hard in the audiovisual sector, but it was not part of a concerted strategy and never made it off the ground.

There is no doubt that a new negotiating round will materialize in several years. We will then see whether the Americans and Europeans can succeed in opening markets for services. That will depend on the respective strength of the trade partners. In other words, if the Far East at that time has been able to gain a sufficiently strong foothold in the service sector, it may happen; otherwise, it will be very difficult.

The prospect for opening up the markets for the service sector is to be found in quite another strategy. The problem with the Uruguay Round was that it was a global negotiating round. Everything was included, and everything depended upon everything else. Various sectors were held hostage to other sectors. That mistake hopefully will not be repeated next time. The way ahead is to take one segment of world trade and negotiate between the interested partners. By doing this, services and well-defined sectors inside services may be liberalized.

The enterprises will undoubtedly make their influence felt. Since they see the world as a global market and since they see the emerging freedom to localize, they will not want the national states to spoil these opportunities by raising or maintaining any barriers to services. They will signal to the national states that a condition for their presence is liberalization of trade in services.

The third main difference in the trade system is found in the fact that borders have disappeared or will disappear in the future. This leaves much more scope for the activity of the enterprises. They can now truly go international. They can operate and choose from among the big international centers. They can play on the new regional pattern including the cross-border regions emerging in Europe. They can link up with a local community if they wish to do so to form a fruitful cultural and social partnership. The door is wide open.

The enterprises may and will certainly use the abolition of political borders and the weakening of the national state to take on a new role. They will gradually appear as power centers themselves. Enterprises will not necessarily take the form of big conglomerates. It is doubtful, in fact, whether such big entities can survive in the future. Witness the fate of IBM, General Motors, and the Ford Motor Corporation. It is much more likely that enterprises will start to play the power game of the national state for the last 200 years and of the European principalities before that: alliances and shifting alliances to exploit opportunities for increased powers which may be of permanent or ephemeral nature. Enterprises may take over as power centers. They will transfer production and research and development from place to place. People may follow in some cases.

The enterprises will play the game according to the established rules, that is, center-hinterland-periphery. They will establish centers from which new ideas will emanate to other regions, to other enterprises, and to other parts of the same enterprise. The center will be a genuine center in the sense that it will not feel any special responsibility for parts of the enterprise not included in the center role. Hinterlands will be built and used so that the center can flourish. For the center, the hinterland is quite simply the hinterland without any established rights or privileges compared to other hinterlands. In a sense, it can be said that centers produced by the enterprises will be much more ruthless than the traditional centers shaped by the old city-states of Europe. The periphery will play its well-known role—not to be envied.

The logical extension of this line of thinking is to see customers, competitors, and staff members as center, hinterland, and periphery. That will happen and is already happening. For customers, it happens when the enterprise decides where to market a new product and where to introduce new service facilities. And where to dump old products. It also applies to production equipment; hinterlands and peripheries may be left with worn-out and out-of-date production technology.

For competitors, it happens according to where the enterprise puts its elite troops in the competitive game. Where do the best managers—the best warriors—go?

For staff, it can be felt with regard to remuneration and training. Some of the staff is relegated to the role of periphery by being asked to leave the enterprise with or without a golden handshake. Note that, with regard to staff, all groups of personnel from the members of the board to the office clerk can fall into all three groups.

The national state may not matter much in such a world. If the state imposes new policies detrimental to the interests of the large enterprises, they may leave the national state or they may change the structure of their alliances to take the new circumstances into account. The balance of payments of individual national states may no longer attract as much attention. The attention will, instead, be focused on the surplus or deficits of the enterprises and alliances.

International integration, as for example European integration, will have a double role. First, it will provide a stable framework for this development exactly as the national state provided a stable framework for industrialization. Second, it will control, if possible, this development exactly as the national state tried to control industrialization.

The power game in the next decade will emerge as a transition from a conventional power game—to divide the world—into a quite unconventional and indeed totally new form. In a large part of the 1990s, we will see the national states or groups of nations, such as the European Union, play a more or less conventional role as competing centers with hinterlands and peripheries. Gradually, the military vector will rest with the United States, the financial and technological vector with Japan and East Asia, and the cultural vector with Europe.

Later in the 1990s, as the world approaches the year 2000, we will see transnational centers (between five and ten) competing with the national states and the European Union for roles as predominant centers. As time goes by, the transnational economic power centers will crowd out the national states.

In the beginning of the next century, the national states will be weakened even more as the transnational enterprises feel their way into the real power game.

On the basis of the following two assumptions—a diminishing role for the military vector and the transition from the industrial age to the information age—the division of the world will no longer be between national states but between (1) transnational economic power centers exercising the traditional role of centers with hinterlands and peripheries in other geographical areas like the old colonial systems and (2) transnational or supranational enterprises exploiting the vacuum left by weak national states in the wake of the globalization of the economy.

7

Europe in the 1990s

THE LESSON OF 1992

Europe in the 1990s is like a ship entering uncharted waters: a lot of excitement but very little knowledge about the destination. 1992 gave Europeans two strong and noteworthy lessons.

The first lesson was a very simple one. Strong forces tried to pull the European Community apart: the Danish and the French referendums on the adoption of the Maastricht Treaty, turbulence on the currency markets, criticism of the Maastricht Treaty in Germany, and revolt against the treaty in the British Parliament. However, at the end of the year when the political leaders met at the Edinburgh European Council (December 11–12, 1992), they decided not only to stick together but to strengthen the integration. Thus the forces holding the European Community together proved to be stronger than both the potential and existing forces pulling it apart. This evolution continued in 1993.

The second lesson was slightly more complicated. Ideas such as transparency and subsidiarity signaled that Europeans do in fact find the union's decision-making procedure increasingly out of step with reality. Transparency means a decision-making procedure in which it can clearly be seen who is responsible and how decisions are being made. Subsidiarity means that the European Union confines itself to objectives that cannot be solved by the member states alone. The voters take the view that the time has come to rethink all or at least part of the decision-making process. They point toward some kind of a missing link between the voters and the politicians making the decisions.

Taken together, these two lessons mark a somewhat different course for the European Union than what seemed most likely when the Treaty of Maastricht was signed on February 7, 1992.

Barring unforeseen events, the institutional process toward a European Union will be continuous rather than discontinuous. It is not likely that we will see a grand and pompous gathering paving the way for a treaty once and for all solving all institutional questions. For all vectors—membership, institutional structure, substance of the integration, and relations to third countries—we are much more likely to see a gradual and evolutionary development, one in which Europeans will shape some kind of common attitude.

There are several scenarios which are very unlikely. Europe is not going to develop into some kind of United States of Europe. Some Europeans favor that course; others do not. All the signs, not the least of which is the history of Europe, indicate that this is not likely to occur. It would remove too many of the fundamental differences between the European nations and the European peoples. It simply is not in the spirit of Europe. The days when the supporters of federation fought the supporters of confederation belong to the past. This philosophical question may still raise the temper of a good many people, but it is not dominating the political agenda of Europe. There is no reason to fight over such words when it becomes increasingly clear that the European construction will not follow any of the well-known, well-defined models.

The new Europe will not be a new kind of superpower, certainly not in the military area. Europeans do not want that. The days when Europeans sallied forth to conquer and dominate are over. Europeans may be ready to defend what is theirs and what they see as their legitimate interests, but nothing more. They do not want to emulate the Americans who have developed the potential to project power over a considerable part of the globe.

We should look for a new European model adapted to European needs and based upon European conditions. The lesson of history shows unequivocally that European integration has gone deep and fast when based on economics, technology, trade, and culture. Every time the military vector has been brought into play, the venture has failed. Napoleon and Hitler are the two latest examples of that. Integration by force simply does not work. It produces a reaction in the form of centrifugal forces that break up the integration enforced by military forces.

Economics, technology, trade, and culture will provide the glue for European integration. They pull different nations and different people together in a loose network connected by spirit instead of force—held together by the will to keep together, by a realization of shared interests and common backgrounds.

Some will argue that the European integration will now run out of steam because the disappearance of the Soviet Union has removed the common enemy that provided the raison d'être. There is something to be said for this viewpoint. History indicates that a threat from outside is a very strong catalyst for integration. Without such a threat, national states may be much less willing to abandon sovereignty. The theory fails, however, to take two things into account.

First, the scaling down of the military vector in the international power game means that the military threat from the former Soviet Union is no longer as important. What matters in the 1990s is the economic and technological threat coming from the United States and Japan. So, in fact, Europe has enemies even if we decline to use that term to speak instead of competitors. The European Council meeting held in Copenhagen in June 1993 devoted most of the time to the economic and technological challenge presented by the United States and Japan. Instead of forecasting the silent death of European integration because of the demise of the Soviet Union, it is more realistic to predict a strong revival of European integration to cope with new economic and technological challenges.

Europeans have begun to realize, with an awful, almost deadly clarity, that the survival of Europe for the next generation will be determined by how well they cope with the double challenge from the United States and Japan, with regard to economic policy and technology, and with the newly industrialized countries, with regard to wage costs.

Second, Europe has always been pulled together or pulled apart by thoughts, ideas, and philosophy, and the Europe now in the offing is not shaped in the mold of a military superpower. The strongest integration in Europe occurred during the medieval period, when the Catholic Church dominated the minds of people. On the basis of common way of thinking (culture), economics, technology, and trade followed producing a strong integration lacking only the political institutions to resemble something like what could be termed a loose confederation/loose federation. Europe was characterized by the free circulation of goods, free passage for persons wanting to travel from one part of Europe to another, and a network among the intellectual elite that wiped away any barriers of the location of one's origin. The members of the intellectual elite shared access to the universities of Europe regardless of geography and political borders, and they communicated easily by writing and by personal appearance. Craftsmen moved from one corner of Europe to any other. People of all kinds took up positions with kings or princes without anyone really paying attention to nationalities.

This is the kind of Europe that is emerging from behind the smoke-screen of the difficult, almost incomprehensible, treaty texts: a loose establishment governed by realities instead of a supreme political body; culture, economics, technology, and trade in the driver's seat; and the integration of everyday life governing the integration with political institutions following behind.

THE ENLARGEMENT OF THE EUROPEAN COMMUNITY/ EUROPEAN UNION

The European Community has gone through three periods of enlargement: in 1973 with the United Kingdom, Denmark, and Ireland (Norway negotiated entry but did not accede following a negative outcome of the referendum); in 1981 with Greece; and in 1986 with Spain and Portugal.

The Europe Union started expansion negotiations with Austria, Sweden, and Finland in February 1993 during the Danish presidency and with Norway less than two months later. The negotiations were brought to a successful outcome a little more than a year later in March 1994, during the Greek presidency. In the beginning of June 1994, an Austrian referendum gave approximately 2/3 in favor of joining the European Union. The four accession treaties were signed at the end of June 1994. Provided that the referendum in Finland (scheduled for October 1994), Sweden (scheduled for November), and Norway (scheduled for November) give a majority for a yes vote, all four EFTA countries can be expected to join the European Union in the beginning of 1995.

Two central points must be answered in this context. The first one is whether the community system must be recast to accommodate the EFTA countries as full members of the European Union. The answer is no. The community institutions and the so-called *acquis communautaire* (the substance of the existing community system) can without much adjustment take into account the EFTA countries. There is no need for any fundamental change. If the European Community could be enlarged from six to twelve member states with countries as different as Denmark, the United Kingdom, and Spain, it is difficult to see why the accession of the EFTA countries should make it necessary to introduce more than technical and administrative amendments. The second point is more interesting. It has been decided that the European Union will assemble another intergovernmental conference in 1996. The question is whether this conference will take place before or after enlargement with at least some of the EFTA countries. Is the European Union ready to let new and untried members influence the shape of the union for the rest of this century, or will the union force them to accept a new and different union instead of the one with which they negotiated? Based on experience in international behavior, the answer is that the European Union will not shut the door for the newcomers to take part in the coming intergovernmental conference. If circumstances prevent entry before the intergovernmental conference starts, a formula will be found to solve the problem of timing, but the most likely outcome is that enlargement will take place before the intergovernmental conference convenes.

That will make the European Union a club of at most sixteen members in the middle of the 1990s.

The next group of countries knocking on the door comprises the Central and Eastern European countries. These countries have already negotiated association agreements with the union. We can probably envisage a process constituted of several stages.

The first stage is already taking place: the association agreements and the efforts being made to improve these agreements. This was decided at the European Council meeting held in Edinburgh on December 11–12, 1992. The idea is to prepare four countries—Poland, the Czech Republic, the Slovak Republic, and Hungary (the Visegrad countries)—for future membership. This stage will last several years during which membership is not a realistic possibility. The countries in question do not possess the economic, industrial, and social structure that would make them eligible for membership in the early 1990s.

At the meeting of the European Council held in Copenhagen in June 21–22, 1993, the road toward membership for the Central and Eastern European countries was mapped out. Decisions were taken with regard to a political dialogue and improved trade relations.

Sometime in the middle of the decade, the Central and Eastern European countries will pose their candidature in earnest for membership (formal application may be forthcoming earlier). It is too early to say whether the answer from the European Union at that juncture will be yes or no. It depends, of course, on the developments that occur from now until that time. Provided that the reform process produces another economic and social structure—which is possible, maybe even likely—we can expect negotiations for enlargement to begin after the conclusion of the next intergovernmental conference held in 1996. These negotiations may be more difficult than the negotiations undertaken with the EFTA countries. More and longer transitional arrangements will be demanded.

The vital question, however, has nothing to do with enlargement itself, but it is a question of fundamental importance to the European Union. It is possible that only a minor adjustment will be made to the system itself in the wake of the enlargement with the EFTA countries. Will the same be true for the system after enlargement with the Central and Eastern European countries? Some people have already said that it is not possible. To our mind, that is too rash. It depends on the evolution of the European Union, and it depends, more than anything else, on the ambitions and the outcome of the next intergovernmental conference to be held in 1996. How can anybody say that the European Union existing after that conference cannot accommodate the Central and Eastern European countries, when no one knows what kind of European Union will emerge from these negotiations? The more centralized the union, the less likely it is that the Central and Eastern European countries can be accommodated. The less centralized the union, the more likely it is. In view of the fact that European evolution is running toward decentralization, it is by no means a foregone conclusion what will happen to the structure of the European Union when it comes of age in the second half of the decade.

This also means that the intergovernmental conference scheduled for 1996 takes on a meaning other than that envisaged in the Maastricht Treaty. It is likely that the main theme will be what amendments in the substance and which institutional reforms are required to accommodate the Central and Eastern European countries as members. In the end, most people would agree that the EFTA countries could join without much change to the community system; not many people would agree to that statement when talking about the Central and Eastern European countries.

At the end of the decade, the European Union may comprise as many as twenty (maybe even twenty-five) member states. It may or it may not be a multispeed community. The Central and Eastern European member states may not participate in all aspects of the union, but the same may be true for such countries as the United Kingdom and Denmark (as it is today in some respects). The more we accept the idea of an integration based on culture, economics, technology, and trade, the more likely it is that we will see a loose integration that does not impose exactly the same status on all members in the union.

This leaves the Southern European countries who have applied for membership: Turkey, Cyprus, and Malta. The community has already decided to do something for these countries, but it has not decided to do what these countries want the community to do: Give the green light for membership. All of them have valid claims for accession to the community, but it is also true that all of them pose obstacles. In the case of Turkey, it is difficult to know whether the Turkish economy is ready to assume the obligations accompanying membership; furthermore, Turkey's relations to Greece are in question. Cyprus reflects the Turkish-Greek dispute. Malta is a so-called ministate.

These obstacles will not necessarily prevent one or more of these countries from becoming members of the European Union; however, they do pose a more difficult political and economic problem for the community than did the EFTA countries and probably more than the Central and Eastern European countries. It is doubtful that any of these countries will have joined the community before the end of the decade.

The three Baltic States—Estonia, Latvia, and Lithuania—have a trade and partnership agreement with the community. At the meeting of the European Council held on June 21–22, 1993, in Copenhagen, it was decided that these agreements should be amended into free trade agreements. It was added that association agreements were the objective. If one or more of the Central and Eastern European countries succeed in entering the European Union, the Baltic States may begin to entertain the idea of joining the European Union.

This development is not without important security aspects. The three Baltic States have seceded from the Soviet Union, but they are, by geography, neighbors of the still mighty Russia. There is a large minority of Russians in each of the Baltic States (primarily in Estonia and Latvia). Kaliningrad is squeezed in as an enclave between Poland and Lithuania. An old-style bilateral political system in this part of Europe carries the seeds of conventional conflict provoked by the minorities and in an area of one national state encapsulated by other national states. The only way to solve this problem is to multilateralize the region politically and economically. The only instrument that can perform the transition from bilateralism to multilateralism is the European Union. It would be wise to try to make the three Baltic States catch up with the four Visegrad countries with regard to membership in the European Union.

Slovenia and Albania have also concluded trade and partnership agreements with the community. Slovenia may fall into a category eligible for membership in the not too distant future. It does in fact already fulfill most of the obligations and could possibly join the community during the 1990s.

Finally, the question arises about Romania and Bulgaria. These two countries have an association agreement much along the same lines as those of the four Visegrad countries, but they are not fully comparable to the Visegrad countries. It is unlikely that they can follow the Visegrad countries toward membership in the European Union in the same timetable.

THE INSTITUTIONAL SYSTEM OF THE EUROPEAN UNION

The Maastricht Treaty is difficult to read, even more difficult to understand, and the task of explaining it is most arduous. It is necessary to grasp three essential factors.

First of all, approximately 80 percent of the political establishment in all member states endorse and support the Maastricht Treaty, but it is supported by only half of the voters in Denmark and France, and it is being questioned in the United Kingdom and to a certain extent in Germany. Apparently, there is some kind of dichotomy between the politicians and the people.

The answer is that the politicians, but not the people, have grasped that the majority of the problems faced by the European nations in the 1990s are international in character and accordingly require international solutions. The politicians recognize that national sovereignty is becoming an empty shell. Most of the problems faced by the national states cannot be solved by the national states alone. They prefer to give up a large part of their sovereignty in order to influence the decisions taken in an institutionalized framework for the integration—the institutions of the European Community which, in the course of 1993, was replaced by the European Union. If this were not true, the politicians would be left out in the cold with diminishing influence on the destiny of their electorate. The future of Europe would be left to market forces, not governed by political directions and not under the control of national or European legislation. We have no doubt whatsoever that the European integration process will continue during the 1990s with an increasing pace. Nor is there any doubt that European politicians will try to govern that process.

In the second place, the Maastricht Treaty does not contain a single major policy item, which was typical of its predecessors. The ECSC treaty of 1952 focused on coal and steel. The Treaty of Rome of 1958 was built around common agricultural policy and the customs union for industrial goods. The main instrument was the principle of nondiscrimination. The Single Act of 1986 introduced the single market. All of these treaties were simple to understand and simple to explain.

The Maastricht Treaty suffers from the difficulty that it was negotiated when the two apparently contradictory currents of economic internationalization and cultural decentralization entered the European scene. Even if it did not say it explicitly and even if few of the negotiators used these terms, the treaty embodies these two currents. The economic and monetary union is the clearest example of economic internationalization. Introduction of cultural decentralization is primarily reflected by subsidiarity. However, it is also clearly seen in several articles, which state that the European Union only supports or supplements what the member states themselves are doing. With regard to culture itself, it is remarkable that the relevant article section XVI explicitly recognizes cultural differences among member states.

All this is laudable; however, it poses difficulties when one is facing an audience trying to explain what the treaty means. It is no simple task. It is so complicated that many people—even some who actually favor these ideas—give up and decide to vote against the treaty just to play it safe.

Third, the treaty is a mixture of supranational items and ordinary intergovernmental cooperation, but both are being put together in one treaty. The amendments to the original treaty are inscribed in the supranational framework; common foreign and security policy plus legal matters (for example, immigration) are intergovernmental. That blurs the issues. Many find it difficult to understand that common foreign and security policy is still based upon intergovernmental cooperation when it is incorporated into a treaty together with the original Treaty of Rome.

On top of that, the treaty contains provisions that take effect immediately as well as policy orientations to be approved and implemented at a later date. Amendments to the Treaty of Rome—qualified majority voting for the protection of the environment and for a number of issues covered by the so-called social dimension—take effect from the day the treaty enters into force. But items such as the third stage of the economic and monetary union plus defense policy and defense itself are issues to be decided upon at a later date. With regard to the third stage of the economic and monetary union, it is explicitly mapped out what it means, but it is still left for later decision to implement the third stage. With regard to defense policy and defense itself, these are defined as objectives for the member states but it is not only left for later decision, it is also left for a later date to define what these objectives mean. It is not completely wrong to say that a major part of the Maastricht Treaty consists of political objectives to be decided upon and to a certain extent also filled in by member states at a later date.

The interregnum from 1993 to 1996 (the next intergovernmental conference) will see no major changes in the institutional structure of the European Union. The basic distribution of competences between the institutions of the European Union will be maintained. The balance of powers between the member states (most clearly seen by the rules for majority voting) will not be changed. The blurred picture of distribution of objectives and instruments between the institutions of the European Union and the member states will continue to be blurred albeit it will be much regretted.

Transparency and subsidiarity will certainly be incorporated into the decision-making procedures of the European Union. That can be done within the existing framework on the basis of the decisions from the European Council meetings held in Birmingham and Edinburgh during the second half of 1992.

The main problem for the European Union is to establish an unbroken link from the voters to the politicians responsible for decisions in the European Union. That is the case for the democratic system working in individual member states. Voters do have a clear idea of which politicians are responsible for which decisions on a national and local level. They can punish or reward politicians by the ballot box. The system works. That was not the case for the system in the European Community, and it is not the case for the system in the European Union. The distribution of powers between the national state and the union is blurred. The institutions in the European Union do not work in a way that makes it clear what exactly they are doing. The commission makes proposals, but it is not responsible for decisions. They are being taken by the council but often by majority voting, which means that a minister from a member state having voted against a measure does not feel responsible for the decision. That is little help for any of the minister's voters who are not satisfied with the decision. The European parliament is not a real parliament. It has limited powers and, for most legal acts, it pronounces its view, but it is up to the council to decide. So, the voter in the national state who wishes to penalize or reward a politician for a decision finds it extremely difficult to know who exactly is responsible. That is not a good omen for a democratic system. Correcting this problem is one of the most important tasks facing the European Union in the future.

One might wonder why this problem arises now as some kind of bolt from the blue. Why has the community system to all appearances lived happily with a system so heavily flawed? Part of the answer is that the community system has dealt primarily with matters that do not attract the attention of the public. The competences given to the community institutions did not go beyond what was considered normal for the system as it was designed. The second part of the answer is that both the community system and the surrounding world have grown up, and that is why this problem now comes to the surface.

First, legislation becomes more and more complicated and more and more sophisticated. This is the case on the national level, where the political establishment strives to keep pace with developments. Regardless of the efforts made, national legislation becomes more complicated every day. This legislation, however, is firmly anchored in the national state, and unreadable law texts do not attract the attention of the public. The public has become used to it. But the public does react to community legislation because something new attracts their attention. They are not used to it.

Second, there is no clear distribution of competences between the European Community or the European Union and the member states. It is difficult for citizens to understand what exactly the community legislation means and what exactly the national legislation is doing. An example of this is the many directives that concern the single market, which lay down the framework but leave the implementation to the national authorities.

Third, the introduction of a common foreign and security policy, plus legal matters such as immigration, completes the picture. The community moves from taking care of the price of pigmeat (pork) to potential discussions concerning not only foreign and security policy, but also—in the long run—defense matters. That gives the European Union yet another dimension in the eyes of the public. The decision-making procedure with checks and balances for fixing the price of pigmeat may not look quite as reassuring when the role of the European Union in the former Yugoslavia is being discussed.

This is where the role of the commission becomes fragile and even vulnerable. The basic idea behind the independence of the commission was that it should make proposals taking into account the interest of the European Community as a whole. That is why it is independent of the national governments. That may be fine when the competence of the commission is confined to economic and trade questions, where some kind of institution may be needed to disregard national interests. But that is not exactly the case and may even be dangerous when the union moves from this sector into the area of foreign and security policy and legal questions. The European public may find it odd if a nonelected body influences decisions that influence the civil war in the former Yugoslavia or deal with the question of receiving refugees in the member states.

To a certain extent, questions of this kind were put forth by France and several other countries during the Uruguay Round negotiations. The commission negotiates on behalf of the European Community and its member states. The negotiations take place in a framework, where it is completely up to the Commission to decide, whether, and to what extent, the member states shall be informed. Some member states put the question whether they can live with a system that gives the commission, which is not answerable to the voters, such powers to the detriment of the member states which are indeed answerable to the voters. In other words, the member states have to defend the decisions taken by the commission sometimes without their knowledge and sometimes against their wishes. They even have to meet the voters and defend the commission negotiators. When being asked by the voters how the result was achieved they will have to rely on the explanations given to them by the commission.

When one recalls these observations, it is remarkable that the European Union succeeded in concluding the Uruguay Round. Beneath the surface, the forces that hold the member states together are extremely strong. Looked at from the outside, the centrifugal forces certainly appeared to be strong enough to jeopardize the whole venture. But when the decision was due, the union once again decided to stick together and to overcome any difficulties. The Uruguay Round is an interesting example precisely because it foreshadowed the transition from the old community system, dealing almost exclusively with industrial and agricultural questions, to the European Union, extending its powers into the area of foreign and security policy. That is why the criticism voiced by several member states is an omen of the criticism that will arise if the European Union continues to use the existing decision-making procedure in such new areas as foreign and security policy and legal matters.

The European Community or the European Union is in transition from an almost exclusive economic integration to a more complex European network. This notion of transition is borne out by the fact that there must now be a clearly defined distribution of competences among the European level, the national level, the regional level, and the local level. Such a distribution of competences has never previously been necessary because the community system was geared to a well-defined—and limited——economic integration.

Some of the problems facing European politicians and consequently also the European populations come from the fact that the Maastricht Treaty opens the door to such a distribution of competences among different layers in the decision-making pyramid. It is not only interesting as a theoretical exercise, but it has wide and far-reaching political consequences. In fact, a political process can mature only when it recognizes this problem and comes to grips with it. And this is just what the European Union has started to do.

On the European level, we see such items as common foreign and security policy, a large part of the economic and monetary policy, a large part of the industrial and technology policy, plus a common trade policy. In these sectors, member states have decided not to exercise competences on the national level, but to take and implement decisions in common respecting agreed rules and procedures.

The whole philosophy first of the European Community and then of the European Union has been to refrain from any measures having harmful or detrimental effects on neighbors. In the Treaty of Rome, this principle was confined to economic policy, industrial and agricultural policy, and trade policy. The Single Act of 1986 and, more significantly, the treaty of the European Union of 1992 extend this principle into the area of foreign and security policy. Without this principle explicitly laid down in the treaties and followed by member states not questioning its validity the whole community system would fall apart.

On the national level is a large scope of sectors, in which the member states have kept powers exclusively to themselves. The member states can maintain or improve social welfare, and the member states can decide distribution of income. A large part of the education sector (first of all, primary schools) falls into this category.

An interesting but also dangerous area are those sectors in which powers can be distributed both on a European level and on a national level. That happens in a large part of the industrial policy, exactly where we find many of the examples used to demonstrate a blurred decision-making process. In this sector, in the years to come, the European Union must embark upon the tedious task of distributing powers more clearly.

On the regional and local levels, it is mainly up to the member states themselves to decide how much decentralization they want. The tendencies go toward more decentralization. The European Union gives a push in that direction. This is borne out by the developments in Germany, where the German *Länder* play a more significant role.

Most democracies are based upon a bicameral system. The British Parliament is composed of an upper house and a lower house. The Congress of the United States is composed of the Senate and the House of Representatives. In France, we have the Senate and the Assembly; in Germany, the Bundestag and the Bundesrat.

The community system apparently is not a bicameral system but based upon one institution that makes decisions: the Council. This assumption is, however, not completely correct. When we look closer at the system we can see that it is indeed a bicameral system or rather it is, in theory, built as a bicameral system. The equivalent of the U.S. Senate is the Council in which the national states or the national governments are represented. The equivalent of the House of Representatives is the European Parliament, in which the people of Europe are represented. This model seems more theoretical than real because most of the powers for decision making are vested in the Council. In these circumstances, it does not give much meaning to talk about a bicameral system, although it is an embryonic bicameral system in which the institutions for such a system are in place.

This sketch would be much more apparent if or when the decision to share powers more equitably between the Council and the European Parliament were ever taken. The fact that this decision has not yet been taken, in spite of more than forty years of integration since the entry into force of the European Coal and Steel Community, means that this is not necessarily what will materialize. Europe, compared to the United States, has at least one major difference and that is its old, well-established regions. So, while it makes much sense to talk about a clear bicameral system in the United States, it is by no means a foregone conclusion in Europe.

In this respect, the Treaty of European Union introduces one new factor: a regional committee. It has less power than the European Parliament. It can only pronounce an opinion, and that not even in all cases, before the European Union makes a decision. But in this as in many other situations what may matter is the beginning—the introduction of something new. This committee did not appear in the old community system. It is the invention of the Treaty of European Union, which, incidentally, in our opinion is also a treaty that introduces decentralization and regionalization on the European level.

This new committee may have far-reaching consequences for the evolution of the decision-making process in Europe for the next decade or two. Let us start by asking whether the national states or the regions will be represented in the part of the bicameral system that encompasses the member states. As it is now, the answer is the member states. In the 1990s, the answer may gradually be both. It may well be the case that the regions will seize the chance they have been given to influence the decision-making model much more than envisaged. While it is still natural to see the European Parliament as the representative of the peoples on the European level, two different bodies may compete to represent the national states: the member states and the regions. The logical continuation of this line of thought is to see a European model developing not toward a bicameral system but toward a tricameral system.

1. The European Parliament representing the people on the European level. This may happen when the national parliaments take on a much more distinct role in European affairs. There is no saying that the national parliaments should abandon their powers automatically to the European Parliament. It may well be the case that parliaments on the national level and the European level will work out some kind of modus vivendi either by distribution of powers or by a rather complicated system of shared powers.

However, the scales may tip the other way. One of the institutional battles during the 1990s may be between the European Parliament and the national parliaments. The national parliaments are gearing up for more influence on European policy in the coming years. Until now, conventional wisdom said that this was designed to exercise control over national governments so as to curb the power of the Council. But, it may also be used against the European Parliament if that institution tries to grab some of the powers invested in the national parliaments. Such an institutional battle may be extremely interesting to watch. Almost all other historic constitutional struggles have been fought between kings and parliaments, not among parliaments.

The problem is that the European Parliament has never really succeeded in getting through to people. It has never fulfilled the proper role of a parliament—it has never constituted a link between lawmakers and their constituencies. That may or may not happen in the future. For the European Parliament, the crucial test may come in the next period, which is from June 1994 to June 1999. If it does not make a breakthrough during that five-year period it may lose momentum. Apparently the distance, measured not only in geographical terms, from the electorate to the European parliamentarians is too great. Because of the complexity of European legislation the European parliamentarians get bogged down in technicalities and lose their true and proper role. The term "technocratic parliament" has been used occasionally to describe this situation.

2. The Council representing the member states or the national states. The Council will, by all accounts, continue to be the main decision-making institution, but some adjustments will probably be made to its current powers and current role. In such a tricameral system, this body

could possibly be entrusted with the power to exercise some kind of veto over proposals that go too far too fast. The Council is a safeguard against an unwarranted undermining of the existing powers of the national states.

3. The Regional Committee representing the regions or the decentralized units of the national states. This body could gradually make its weight felt in the decision-making process and exercise it in common with the European Parliament and the national parliaments.

It may also be that the regions will directly attack the prerogative of the member states to exercise European policy. That is the case in Germany. During the ratification of the Treaty of European Union, the German *Länder* managed to increase their influence on Germany's European policy. That could be an omen for what will come in the future, not only in Germany, but also in many other European national states with strong regions.

It may not have been the intention, but we may see alliances between regions from different member states making their impact on the union's decision-making system. Especially among the large member states the discussion in the Council masks disagreement inside such a member state. That may now come out into the open by the good offices of the Regional Committee. Regions worried, for example, about the environment might form alliances regardless of which member states they belong to. If such building of alliances starts to gain momentum, the Regional Committee could really change decision making in the union. If it happens, it will point strongly toward some kind of tricameral system with the Regional Committee and the regions themselves in a much stronger role than envisaged. From time to time, history provides examples of something new bringing about much more far-reaching changes than intended. Maybe we have such an example here.

As a long shot, we could also envisage an enhanced role for the Economic and Social Committee. This body has not had much influence in the community life. That may change. In the future, it may force its way into influencing decision making.

This institutional model is consistent with our thinking about the evolution of the European integration process. The appearance of the region and, in particular, the cross-border region needs to be intercepted by the institutional system. The enterprise and the trade unions as cultural factors must also be reflected in the institutional system.

The conclusion is thus that even if we start out by seeing some strong similarities to the American bicameral model (and the British model) we finish by sketching a totally different one taking into account the stronger role of the regions and the enterprises plus the trade unions in the years to come.

The main problem facing the European Union is how to deal with an institutional jigsaw puzzle. In the real world, power does not respect conventional borders. Power no longer rests primarily with one body and one only, for example, the national state. On the contrary, it is fragmented. In some areas the national state is still the dominant body, but in other areas regions, or cross-border regions, or transnational enterprises, or some other official or semiofficial body, possibly even a private body are the real powers. When the average citizen is asked to whom he or she defers, there is no longer a simple answer. The citizen may not even really know. It depends on the issue and the location under consideration. That is why well-known and well-established power structures inside the national state are under attack and that is why the European integration process faces problems unknown a few years ago.

Not only does the citizen have to think of three, four, or five bodies when being asked who is governing everyday life, often these bodies have powers that overlap. And that is the crucial issue: overlapping powers. In some areas, the European Union and the national state introduce legislation; in other areas, the national state and the transnational enterprises grab for powers governing everyday life.

There is no easy answer to the question of how to shape a new institutional framework taking these factors duly into consideration. That is why the model incorporated in the Maastricht Treaty is neither lucid nor logical. That is also why the model outlined above suffers from the same lack of clarity. We are groping in the dark. We are trying to cut through the maze and figure out how to solve the problem of overlapping powers between different institutions and various bodies not incorporated in the old European system built after the Napoleonic wars on the basis of the industrial age. For the moment, we can probably do no better than to provide channels for the forces visible hoping that the mist will evaporate and some day we will be able to see more clearly.

In this perspective, the ongoing debate about the weight of the smaller vis-à-vis the larger member states becomes less significant. Weight is not the main question because the national states themselves are witnessing a change in their own influence. In the short run, the political question will probably be solved by refraining from fundamental changes in the institutional system and thus *grosso modo* maintaining the balance between the large and the small member states. It is a nonstarter to look forward to an enlargement of the community while telling newcomers that the community will change the rules so that they will have less influence than they do under the existing rules.

The main point here is a totally different one. How do the European Community and the European Union ensure that small peoples, not necessarily small national states, can maintain their identity and their singular culture? In other words, how will the European Union avoid the cultural imperialism that killed the Soviet empire from within and now eats away at the Anglo-Saxon culture? That question has nothing to do with the members of the institutions and the procedural rules, including voting rights; it is concerned with the right to use the mother tongue, the right to choose religion, and the right to choose schools and other learning facilities. In short, the main question is not on the agenda for current discussions about decision-making procedures in the European Union, but it will be in a few years. It is more than debatable whether the large European national states are the friends of the individual and, in particular, the small peoples of Europe.

The idea of European citizenship is supported by some, contested by others, and feared by some. It is unlikely that Europe will ever see a genuine European citizenship that gives equal rights and equal obligations to all Europeans regardless of where they live. It is much more likely that European citizenship will adopt some kind of dichotomy.

One part will guarantee citizens from all member states certain basic rights. This is already the case for free movement of labor. As a follow-up to the Single Act of 1986, three directives were adopted sketching the conditions for taking up residence in other member states. Quite interestingly, this right was not given automatically. Among other things, the citizen taking up residence in another member state must be able to pay for his or her own living; a citizen from one European country cannot live on social security from the member state chosen for residence.

Another part of European citizenship will reserve certain rights in each member state (or each region or local community) for citizens of that member state. The door for that approach was opened by the Treaty of Rome which reserves some kinds of jobs in the public sector for citizens of the said member state. In many member states, there is a strong reservation about the purchase of secondary residences by citizens from other member states. Rules covering these areas, or at least imposing certain conditions, may well be written into the next treaty. Such an approach—reserving some rights for citizens originating from the member state/region/local community—would underline diversity and respect for individual identities. Switzerland has, for many years, applied a system in which local citizens enjoy certain privileges, ones that are not automatically extended to citizens holding a Swiss passport. The need to take separate regions and individual peoples more into account falls neatly into line with this kind of thinking.

When the Maastricht Treaty was written not very many thought that the idea of citizenship would pose a problem. It was primarily a Spanish and a Portuguese phenomenon due to the considerable number of workers from these two countries living in other member states. However, in the final version of the treaty the citizenship got a presentation which conveyed (incorrectly) the impression that European citizenship meant that the existing national citizenship was being replaced by a European citizenship. This was neither the idea nor the case. The European Union should think twice before touching upon something which apparently is untouchable—national citizenship. The right approach would be to focus upon the rights of citizens which is the real issue.

To sum up, the following items must be respected if the European construction is to be successful: (1) language and religion in all parts of Europe, no matter how small; the European Union must guarantee survival of all languages and religions; (2) national minorities and their ways of life; the people of Europe must be convinced that the European Union will never repress the lifestyle of any minority but will support them all; (3) diversification so that peoples, or regions, may choose their own ways without worrying that they might be forced into some common framework.

THE SUBSTANCE OF THE EUROPEAN UNION

The single market was almost completely established by the beginning of 1993 (the target date). Most community legislation is in place. Most, but not all, of the legislation has been transformed into national legislation. Some aspects of the single market should be accelerated, but *grosso modo* Europe has arrived according to 1985's plan and according to the timetable. It is not always appreciated just how much effort and political willpower this accomplishment has entailed.

Some people tend to see the single market as an exercise in simple arithmetic. The disappearance of trade barriers will, in an econometrical model, stimulate economic growth by about 1 percent, or not much. Our position is that such an approach is more or less irrelevant. What matters are the dynamic aspects. What will it mean to growth, investment, and efforts in research and development? Most analyses conducted to determine the reason for the United States' strong position in high technology during the postwar period point to the large American market. If these findings are correct—and it seems that they are—the same will be true for Europe. In fact, the single market is the European counterattack to win back market shares lost to Japan and the United States during several decades, not by putting up protective barriers against these countries, but by increasing the competitiveness of European companies.

When the idea of the single market was introduced, there was widespread fear in the United States and Japan that the objective was not confined to a single market, but included measures to strengthen community preferences with regard to imports from nonmember states. These fears have been proven to be without foundation. Indeed, no such measures were part of the negotiations for the Single Act, and no member state put forward any ideas to this effect. The basic idea was to strengthen the competitiveness of European industry, not to protect European industry against products from abroad.

Even more important in the long run is the impetus the single market gives to the cooperation necessary among European enterprises. Only the large enterprises have the financial means and the human resources to define the strategy. The small and medium-sized enterprises need access to capital and human resources. They need to join forces with other European enterprises. The single market will be, and already is, the catalyst for this development. It is seen in large countries, such as Germany and France, and in small countries, such as Denmark.

Infrastructure seems to be a new keyword in the European construction. It was brought to the forefront during the meeting of the European Council held on June 21–22, 1993. The conclusions from that meeting reflect increased attention given to the need for building a real European infrastructure. In fact, a modern society cannot function without infrastructure. One of the reasons why the U.S. economy finds it so difficult to take off is that the American infrastructure simply is not adequate. Infrastructure has become one of the parameters of a nation's competitive edge. A bad infrastructure pulls the economy down; an efficient infrastructure pushes it toward high, sustained economic growth.

Infrastructure becomes more and more important as nations move away from the old industrial society toward the immaterial society. Not only do we need to keep traditional infrastructure at a high level, but new needs for infrastructure are forthcoming. The traditional infrastructure was hard; that is, roads, airports, railways, ports, electricity, water, sewage, and so on. These items can be seen and measured, exactly like the industrial goods they help produce. The new infrastructure is increasingly soft—schools, educational facilities for adults, environmental protection, telecommunications, and facilities for exploiting all the new opportunities associated with information technology. Those who grasp this fact will be one step ahead at the beginning of the 21st century. The Europeans may not be quite there, but they are definitely closer to this point than the United States and, probably, Japan.

Indeed, the next big European program, a real challenge for Europeans, may be such an infrastructure program. It would fall neatly into line with the plan for the single market introduced in 1985 and the plan for economic and monetary union mapped out in the beginning of the 1990s. An infrastructure program is one of the most important items in the white paper commissioned by the European Council at its meeting held in Copenhagen in June 1993 and forwarded to the meeting in December 1993 in Bruxelles.

There are many other items in the white paper, but infrastructure is the most tangible item and the one most likely to proceed during 1994. The paper covers many types of infrastructure but focuses upon information technology where it calls for the construction of a European network, one not so different from the one being proposed by President Clinton for the United States.

Such a program for infrastructure not only is an economic phenomenon, but also will have wide-ranging repercussions for the relationships between the public sector and the private sector. For almost twenty years, the privatization program has run ahead leaving a large part of the public sector in search of a new role. The new role will become clear when the need for services and infrastructure makes itself felt as a necessary and unavoidable condition for growth in the growing private sector. Without the infrastructure that can be provided only by the public sector, the benefits of privatization will be short lived. It is logical that this discovery comes to the surface in Europe where the public sector is not looked upon as negatively as it is in the United States.

The White Paper. At the meeting of the European Council held in Copenhagen in June 1993, it was agreed that the commission should forward a white paper for the December meeting of the European Council.

The discussion at the Copenhagen meeting did not go into detail, but it served notice that a substantial policy discussion had begun. The theme was how to reconcile the European welfare societies with economic internationalization bringing about stronger international competition and a global market. It this respect, the discussion begun in Copenhagen can be compared to the breakthrough made in the 1930s that pointed the way toward the welfare society. At that time, the problem was how to do it. Now the problem is how to maintain the system, or rather whether the system can be maintained and which policies will be required to maintain it.

The European national states must meet that challenge now because of the emergence of new competitors. Until a few years ago, Europe's main competitors were the United States and Japan, and the competition was concentrated primarily in one sector: high technology. Now other competitive threats appear not only on the horizon but also on the very doorstep of the Western European economies: low-wage industries undercutting Western European industry without dumping. It is very simple. Wages there are lower than they are in Western Europe and so is productivity, but the productivity gap is smaller than the wage gap. Western Europeans need some time to understand that they were not given the privilege of high real wages by the good God because they are Europeans but because they have had a higher productivity. So, the problem is whether Europeans can maintain a sufficiently high lead in productivity to safeguard and support the high real wages in Europe.

For Europe, this problem is particularly difficult because some of the new competitors are not to be found in the Far East or South Asia but right on the doorstep of Western Europe: The new countries in Central and Eastern Europe have left the Soviet empire and are now trying hard to establish market economies.

Very sensibly, the first European response was to analyze how to restructure the European economies to maintain their present economic strength and provide the necessary financial backing for the welfare state. The answer proposed by the white paper is, not surprisingly, to reduce the low-wage sectors of the international economy and to concentrate on high technology and the service sectors. A larger opening of markets for services in the Uruguay Round would have benefited Europe. That had indeed been the European position for several years, but the attempt was thwarted by the American position after 1990 which gave lower priority to this objective.

The next step is to determine how to reduce or, at least, diminish some of the rigidities in the European labor market. That is a task not only for labor itself but also for the business sector. A parallel effort by labor and business is required. Here Europe may have a competitive edge on the Americans but not on the Japanese.

The third step is to determine whether the welfare state could be adjusted. Is everything invested in the safety net equally important when all European national states feel the financial squeeze? The answer may well turn out to be no with the inevitable result that some adjustment will be required.

Two conclusions can be drawn. First of all, most Europeans and most European national states are committed to the welfare state. Not everybody subscribes to exactly the same model with the same social benefits, but most subscribe to the principles of the model. The objective is to safeguard as much of the model as possible. It is still a widespread opinion that the European economies, even after some trimming and some restructuring, are strong enough to shoulder the burden. That is probably correct provided that fine-tuning with regard to economic policies, monetary policies, restructuring, and trade policies all succeed. There may be some room to maneuver, but it is very narrow indeed. Judged at from the beginning of 1994, Europe is broadly speaking progressing on the right path, but it is still not certain—far from it—that Europe will be successful.

Second, this analysis, discussion, and ultimately policy making can be made only at the European level. This is where we see the real breakthrough with regard to thinking and perception. A few years ago, most people would have said that such a discussion was not for the European level but for the national level. Today, however, it is generally agreed that, if the problems can be solved at all, it can be done only on the European level. In a way, this is the first great test for the European Union. If it can provide some answers and some policies that can show, to the individual, that the European Union can succeed in this, much of the scepticism in Europe toward the European Union will fade away. The fact that the European Union was able to negotiate as an entity in the Uruguay Round gives some hope of this.

It can safely be said that the white paper will be one of the determining factors in the future of Europe. It will determine the political discussions in Europe for years to come, and by so doing, it will set the political agenda.

The Common Agricultural Policy (CAP), probably the most well-known policy of the European Community, has been criticized heavily from abroad and sometimes also from within. The criticism concentrates on the fact that the CAP boosts production bringing about a large surplus of agricultural goods. This criticism is, to a certain extent, justified. The principles behind the CAP are good enough, but prices have been set at a level that makes it profitable to produce in regions such as Bavaria, where natural conditions do not favor agricultural production. The excessively high prices have made it enormously profitable to increase production in such regions as parts of France, the Netherlands, Denmark, and parts of Britain.

The main problem is that it has not been possible to decide whether the CAP is an agricultural policy or a social and regional policy. The fact that it is being implemented to maintain farmers in remote regions for noneconomic reasons has distorted the policy.

If we take a long look at the development of the Common Agricultural Policy, it seems that its problems cannot be solved outside an environmental framework. The farmers want to stay in the countryside cultivating their farms. Politicians want the countryside to be populated. People want the landscape to look orderly. All these objectives converge to a solution where we redefine the role of some but not all farmers. In the future, farmers in remote areas or holiday areas may earn their living not by growing cereals or raising cattle but by looking after the environment. Instead of paying them to produce agricultural goods which nobody wants to buy society may pay them to safeguard the landscape.

Many farmers in such areas have resisted any aid not related to production saying that all they want is a decent price for their products. In other words, they want to earn a living because they work, not to receive social welfare to prevent them from working, from producing farm products. That viewpoint is understandable. We cannot disregard the strong cultural and sociological attachment to the soil. All of us have links to the farming society, but we all have even stronger links to nature. Maybe the circle can be squared by changing the role of some European and American farmers into wardens of nature for future generations.

That would enable efficient farms to produce the agricultural products we all need at a lower price, thus saving consumers and the state budget from supporting inefficient farmers. The Common Agricultural Policy would finally be exactly that—an *agricultural* policy—and nothing else.

The social dimension is another political vector of strong importance for European industries in the 1990s. Its main objective is to ensure that the advantages gained by the single market are not allocated exclusively to industry, entrepreneurs, and shareholders. The workers (the staff) must have their fair share; otherwise, there will be nothing in it for them, and support for the single market will wane away.

The social dimension is based on an idea built into many European countries since the 1930s and the publication of the Beveridge report in Britain in the 1940s. No modern industrial state can survive unless there is a certain amount of social consensus and a reasonable distribution of income and wealth.

Looking at it from the viewpoint of the 1990s, some other, possibly more interesting, aspects can be found. The labor force of the 1990s is not comparable to the labor force of the 1940s. Today we need a highly educated, highly motivated labor force. Productivity is more a question of human resources and less a question of capital. The social dimension reflects the fact that we need to think about the labor force in this way, not as an anonymous mass of grey figures behind machine tools. Enterprises must do a lot for their labor force; otherwise, they will lose the dedication of the staff. The social dimension is one factor that tells us that European industry is moving away from old industrial products into the era of modern high technology and the service industries.

The social dimension has another, quite interesting angle. The United Kingdom did not sign the social dimension and it is therefore not valid in the United Kingdom. That indicates that the United Kingdom wishes to attract labor-intensive industries. That may be profitable in the short run, but, in the long run it will certainly have a detrimental impact on the British economy. Whether people like to hear it or not, this political preference is a clear sign about what kind of industries Britain looks to and which kind of countries Britain sees as its natural competitors. Britain, who gave birth to the Beveridge report, sides in the 1990s with the southern European economies, not with the northern European ones.

The fact that Britain takes a lukewarm attitude toward the European Union makes it necessary for Britain to offer a compensation to industries to keep them on British soil. Every investor is worried about access to the market across the channel. This uncertainty may be compensated for by certain advantages, primarily in the form of lower costs.

These lower costs cannot be found in lower finance costs. The British attitude to the Economic and Monetary Union and the European Exchange Rate Mechanism makes that unlikely. In the short term, financial costs may not be influenced by being in or out, but, in the longer term, it is difficult to escape the conclusion that being out requires some kind of premium.

It has to be found in total labor costs. Because it is difficult and politically complicated to force the wage level down, the British government has chosen to stand outside the social dimension to offer British and foreign enterprises the opportunity of lower nonwage compensation to labor.

This is a dangerous course for Britain to follow because the heart of the matter is that businesses make long-term investment decisions only when a high degree of certainty is available, and that is not the case when access to the European market and certainty about exchange rates and interest rates are not available. (This reasoning lies behind Sweden's decision in 1990 to join the European Community. The decision was made public as the first sentence in a longer economic policy program designed to stimulate growth.) With the enlargement of the union approaching Switzerland outside the European Economic Space seems very odd. The other side of the coin, so to speak, is the argument that the welfare state and nonwage labor costs are putting Europe out of business. Unless the cost level is reduced, European industry may run out of traditional industrial plants in a very short time.

The United Kingdom feels that costs have run out of control. It takes the view that the way ahead, not only for that country but also for the rest of Europe, is to reduce costs. During 1993 that policy, combined with Britain's decision in September 1992 to leave European Exchange Rate Mechanism has stimulated the British economy with a growth rate above the European average.

The crux of the matter in this dispute is not whether one or the other argument can win the day. It concerns the kind of society that is envisaged for the future. There may be something to support the argument for reducing costs—wage and nonwage—if the vision is one of an industrial Europe: a Europe in the mold of the industrial revolution brought up to current standards. If so, Europe should keep costs in rein because all indications are that the competitors are not going to be the Americans and the Japanese but the newly industrialized countries in the Far East (primarily China and India), perhaps Russia, and some Central and Eastern European countries.

The unanswered question in this vision, however, is whether Europe stands any chance whatsoever to win a competitive race of this kind. The odds are not promising. Many Europeans have come to the conclusion that to keep Europe in business engenders a change of parameters away from the industrial society toward the immaterial society. If so, how much effort should be devoted to cost-reducing measures compared with other instruments at our disposal? The social dimension would not be a liability but an asset. It would stress the need to develop human resources, and it points toward shaping a cultural profile of the European enterprises.

Cohesion has become a catchword in the European Community and in the European Union for the last five to ten years. It reflects the basic fact that the old community system was built on the Common Agricultural Policy that favored France and the Customs Union that favored Germany. With the enlargement in the 1980s with Greece (1981) and Spain and Portugal (both in 1986), this system would have produced lopsided effects in that the poorest member countries would not reap their share of the benefits.

The remedy to this imbalance is cohesion: Funds are introduced to transfer money from the richer member states to the poorer member states. These funds are substantial—from 1988 to 1992, 62 billion ECU were transferred; and from 1993 to 1999, 176 billion ECU will be transferred according to the decision of the 1992 Edinburgh meeting of the European Council.

It is, of course, being questioned whether these amounts are working as intended. That is difficult to prove. They do work unquestionably as a political signal that the richer part of the community is ready to help support the poorer part. They are thus not only a part of the so-called *aquis communautaire*, they are, even more important, part of the community solidarity. No state can survive without such a solidarity. No European Union can be built unless solidarity is present and working in a tangible, visible way.

It has been questioned whether cohesion actually works. This is, of course, difficult to prove in statistical terms, but the figures are clear enough. From 1985 until 1992, the gross national product per capita measured against the community average of 100 has increased 7.4 percent in Spain, 4.3 percent in Portugal, and 3.7 percent in Ireland. These three countries seem to be catching up. It is difficult not to attribute some of the responsibility for this development to the transfer of funds from other member states. (For Greece, however, the figures indicate a fall of 4.6 percent.)

There is no doubt that this solidarity will have to be strengthened in the years to come, but the group of members benefiting and paying may change. Italy climbs the ladder and may no longer qualify for help. Britain goes in the opposite direction. In fact, at the end of 1992, Britain was just a few percentage points above the ceiling of 90 percent of gross national product per capita qualifying for assistance under the new cohesion fund. The accession of the EFTA countries will add a group of paying countries to the European Union, possibly at the same time pushing Britain below the 90 percent of gross national product per capita floor.

The European Union budget is a strange animal in the community zoo. It does not have many of the characteristics of the national budgets, nor does it look like the budget of a confederation or federation.

The budget is not an instrument for making economic policy, for example, for influencing the business cycle. Nor is it an instrument for loan transactions, which are usual for a sovereign state. Cohesion means that to a certain, but limited, extent the budget serves as an instrument to distribute income, but it is far too bold to compare it with a national budget. The budget is, nevertheless, an ingenious instrument, which can be understood by looking more closely at the revenue side and the expenditure side.

The revenue side is composed of so-called own resources. The basic idea is that the union is financed by revenue sources linked to the two original common policies: the common agricultural policy (agricultural import levies) and the customs union (customs duties). Later on, 1 percent of a uniform assessment for value-added taxation was introduced. In 1988 a small percentage of the member states' share of the gross national product was added. The pertinent point in all this is that, apart from the last item which accounted for approximately 19 percent of the total revenue in 1992, no effort is envisaged to reflect the economic strength of member states on the revenue side of the budget. In that respect, we are operating with a true community disregarding the size of member states in the financing of common policies.

The expenditure side reveals the same basic idea to disregard the economic strength of member states. The big item has always been the common agricultural policy because it is the only common policy giving rise to community expenditure on a grand scale. The mechanism operates in a way that does not attach importance to where in the community money is actually paid out. Any farmer gets the same price whether he sells to the national market, to other member states, or to nonmember states. That is why it is a common policy; otherwise, it would be linking together twelve national policies. The only policy actually aiming at taking into account where money is really paid out is cohesion, where the objective is to influence income distribution in the community.

The many schemas that demonstrate how the member states are net contributors or net beneficiaries are meaningless because they reflect nonunderstanding of how the budget works and what it really mirrors. Two crucial issues for the budget have already made themselves known during the 1970s and the 1980s and will come to the forefront in the 1990s.

The first issue is the question of whether the budget reflects policy decisions as such taken by the council or whether member states should try to make policy via the budget. Are the common agricultural policy expenditures to be paid out in full in accordance with the legal acts passed by the Council, or should the European Union set a budget ceiling imposing restraints on what the Council can decide? The answer to this highly political question will decide a large part of the future of the European Union. The more we get the answer that policy governs the budget, establishing the budget as an instrument to implement policy and not as a policy instrument in itself, the better are the chances that integration will continue and deepen. The more importance that is placed on the budget, the more likely it is that member states reticent toward integration will stifle it by holding back expenditures. Just as we can read the attitude of the European Union by analyzing the degree of centralization versus decentralization in the national political system, we can read the attitude of the member states toward further integration by finding out whether they see the budget as a mirror for policy decisions or as a policy instrument in itself.

A compromise was worked out during the 1980s. The principal ideas governing the budget were maintained, but on the revenue side a new revenue source, reflecting the economic strength of member states, was introduced while budgetary discipline (mainly directed at the Common Agricultural Policy) was brought into play on the expenditure side. The battle was thus undecided when the European Union was established in 1993.

The second issue concerns the interinstitutional power game. The Treaty of Rome is clear, and the Treaty on the European Union does not change anything in this area. The Council had the most power in decision making. The European Parliament had some limited power. Not surprisingly, the European Parliament tried to increase its powers. For many years, the community was haunted by budgetary crises triggered by disagreements among the institutions. In the period from 1988 to 1993, an armistice was agreed upon by way of an interinstitutional agreement. This agreement was renewed in 1993.

The 1990s will see one other question dominating the budget scene. The European Union will have to decide sooner or later whether the ceiling of 1.27 percent forecast for the total gross national product in the union is sufficient. If the answer is yes, which seems to be the case now, the union will have to recognize that the present budget is too small for a macro-economic instrument because it limits what the European Union can and should do in the future. It may be a very important factor in implementing subsidiarity. It also limits the scope of the union in areas in which many member states would like to see the union play a role: cohesion, financial support of third countries, the environment, research and development, and, of course, continued financing of the common agricultural policy.

A devious way to circumvent difficulties for raising the own resources ceiling would be to work out a distribution of responsibilities between the member states and the union leaving the financing of some semi-common policies to member states. That may be the solution if political considerations bar the way for an outright increase of the financial ceiling, but it would of course not influence total spending. The drawback is that it would further blur the community/union system. In the longer term, it runs the risk of jeopardizing the system itself by transferring financing to the national states.

In the middle of the 1970s, a study group under the leadership of Professor MacDougall[1] came to the conclusion that the community budget in a prefederal stage should be around 2 to 5.5 percent of total community gross national product rising to at least 5 percent in a federation. Sometime during the 1990s the European Union will have to meet that challenge.

Experience clearly shows that control over spending is a crucial item in any state. It took the British Parliament several hundred years to win the battle with the British crown. The United States was just being born when this question was raised more than 200 years ago.

In the construction of the institutional model, the union will have to take into account which powers should be given to which institution. It is more than likely that the newly elected European Parliament in 1994 will not be satisfied with the limited powers bestowed upon the parliament by the treaty, especially not if or when the own resources ceiling is going to be increased. As we approach the stage where the European Union develops into something more than the present beefed up European Community, this question will be one of the most important ones on the agenda. That will be particularly true if or when we come to the point where expenditures vis-à-vis third countries are no longer regarded as a community policy but become part of a common foreign and security policy defined by the European Union. Then the question is who has the right to make decisions of a financial character that have repercussions for the security of the European Union.

At some point during the 1980s, it looked as though the community budget would become a major battleground between the institutions, partly because the European Parliament had given up hope for increased power in the community's legislative process. The European Single Act reversed that trend by associating the European Parliament more closely with the legislative process establishing the single market. Parliament focused again, during the negotiations of the Treaty on the European Union in 1991, on legislative power and got something but not what it wanted. It is a reasonably certain guess that, after having changed its tactics away from the budget to the legislative process with limited success, the European Parliament will swing back toward the budget as a major battleground between the institutions.

The European Economic and Monetary Union will come sooner than most people think. The snag, however, is that it probably will not materialize according to the text in the Maastricht Treaty. As so often has been the case in the history of European integration, substance will precede form. An economic and monetary union will grow out of real integration. It is likely that some kind of link between Germany and France will pave the way. Neither Germany nor France by itself is strong enough to call the tune. Either Europe will abandon the currency battlefield completely—and that is unlikely—or the Germans and the French will find some way to make Europe a player in this game. The message from the events leading up to the debacle of August 1, 1993, is not that a European economic and monetary union is dead. The message is not that the deutsche mark is king, but that it was too weak to support the system in force at that time.

In a few years, there will probably be in Europe something called an economic and monetary union, but it will not necessarily be based on the criteria in the Maastricht Treaty and it will not necessarily comprise all the member states. Then the problem will be twofold. First, what will happen to the European currencies outside this economic and monetary union? The answer is not difficult. They will be sold down the river to speculators. Second, will the core countries of the economic and monetary union accept that? They may be willing to do so in the short run, but it is difficult to see them doing so in the longer run. If this development takes place, the issue of the European economic and monetary union will reemerge as an item for discussion at the next intergovernmental conference scheduled to take place in 1996.

Many Europeans have come to the conclusion that Europe cannot risk the repetition of currency crises every few years. They pose a barrier to economic growth and, at the same time, jeopardize European integration by casting doubt on the political will. Why should Europe leave it to American bankers and Japanese bankers to decide monetary factors in Europe itself?

It cannot be disputed that the broadening of the bands in the ERM system, decided on August 1, 1993, was not a result of objective economic analysis. Already, in February 1993, speculators were trying to force a depreciation of the Danish krone. They were not successful. It is, however, extremely strange to read about economists from big American banks saying that a currency should be depreciated when fundamentals show a surplus on current account corresponding to more than 3 percent of the gross domestic product (GDP) and a prognosis for the coming year pointing upward, the inflation rate down to about 1 to 1.5 percent, and a deficit on public finances less than 4 percent of the GDP. That was what happened to the Danish krone in February 1993.

This was repeated in July when the French franc and the Danish krone were swallowed by the currents of speculation. It has been said that the

European currencies were out of line with competitive parameters and the European governments were foolish to combat the "wise" direction indicated by the market. That is not so. The truth is based upon two things. First, the speculators possess such an enormous potential that they can push any currency over the brink if they so choose. And they make that choice from time to time because they earn money by doing so. By forcing the ERM countries to adjust the system they get a profit. It is pure nonsense to say that the market knows where parities should be and pushes the currencies in that direction. The market knows nothing but tries to make money. Second, the big American banks resent the European economic and monetary union. There is absolutely no doubt that this union will be detrimental for them in the long run. They may have believed that the Europeans would not succeed in building such a union, but when they saw it might be done they knew that it was in their interest to destroy it and that is what they have been trying to do for most of 1992 and 1993. It is not offensive to state this. It is plain fact. Anybody who bothers to look at the figures can see that a European economic and monetary union will harm the interests of American banks. Anybody who knows just a little bit about the currency markets knows that the attack on the ERM was masterminded and carried out by these banks. Time after time, their chief economists called for a realignment of the system. When it had been repeated enough times, it became conventional wisdom.

Some of the reasons behind the support for an economic and monetary union are the same as those for the single market. The dynamic aspects are the most important ones. Investment decisions are not taken in a world of uncertainty. If it is difficult to predict the currency rate some years from now, some enterprises would prefer not to invest. On the other hand, if everybody knows that the exchange rates will be maintained, investment decisions may be implemented.

The European economic and monetary union will be a safeguard against the potential beggar-thy-neighbor policy of the 1990s. The risks are that individual European countries will compete for the savings of the buoyant economies of Eastern Asia. Such a competition will inevitably maintain interest rates at too high a level. The beggar-thy-neighbor policy of the 1990s does not consist of import restrictions, tariffs, or competitive devaluations, but of monetary policies to deprive one's neighbor of access to the savings surplus in other parts of the world. The only method to avoid such a disastrous evolution is the establishment of an economic and monetary union, which will do away with the need for individual member states to maintain their own monetary reserves.

Many economists who have worked with the theory behind economic and monetary unions find it difficult to see how a European economic and monetary union can work. They point to the limited mobility of money, goods, and people that does not fit into such a union. They are correct. That is why the economic and monetary union in Europe will not be like the one existing and working in the United States. The Europeans must replace the factor of mobility, especially the limited mobility of the labor force, with some other adjustment. That role can and will be filled by the enterprises. By close association with regional and local communities, the enterprises will replace some of the adjustment process that is not being performed by labor force mobility.

Again it must be stressed that although some similarities undoubtedly do exist, the European construction should not follow the U.S. pattern. In Europe, there is a totally different tradition for relations between local communities and the enterprises and between the enterprises and their labor forces than there is in the United States. The enterprises in Europe are more interested in keeping the local communities going than are the enterprises in the United States.

It is not surprising that many professional American economists think that the economic and monetary union proposed for Europe is not viable. They only see that the European plan would not work in the United States. The idea, however, is to shape a European economic and monetary union based upon the state of affairs in Europe. The experience gained in Germany in the mid-19th century shows quite clearly that an economic and monetary union can be established and work well for a considerable time without any political integration into a federation. It worked in Germany from the mid-1830s to 1871, and there is no reason why it should not work in Europe during the 1990s and into the beginning of the next century.

The Europeans are fighting a hard struggle against speculators, that is, people who are not convinced that the present policies will be carried out. In 1994 the strongest currency of Europe is not the deutsche mark— far from it. The strongest currencies are the French franc and the Danish krone. Speculators prefer the deutsche mark to these other currencies because they are not convinced that France and Denmark have the political stamina to continue whereas Germany apparently has.

When this battle is won, the war will be won. The speculators will be convinced that the system can and will work, and they will not speculate against it. This battle of conviction—almost a battle of attrition or a battle of will power—was almost won in early summer 1992. When the Danes voted no, a question mark was put on the future of the economic and monetary union. This was enhanced by the scepticism shown in the United Kingdom, Germany, and France. The speculators lost faith in the convergence pushing weaker countries to rein in expenditure on the budget. That launched speculative capital, and the system could not repel such phenomenal sums of money. Had the Danes voted yes, the question remains whether the weak countries would have managed to bring their economic policies under control. If yes, the union would have sailed toward an economic and monetary union in the mid-1990s. If no, the speculation would have surfaced at a later time and probably with more dire consequences for the future of the European Union. The lesson is thus that, for a long time, confidence can carry the system along, but sooner or later the hard realities make themselves felt. Confidence can buy time but it can never be a substitute for the real thing—a sufficient economic and monetary policy on the national level backed by the economic and monetary union.

The protection of the *environment* will certainly be a major theme for the European Union during the 1990s. It fits in nicely with the importance being given to values during the decade leading to the turn of the century.

One of the challenges for Europe is to turn environmental policy into the same kind of general policy that was established, for example, for economic policy. The idea will be to make certain that each time a decision is taken in any area, due consideration is given to all foreseeable repercussions on the environment. Those in charge of the environmental policy will have a say and sometimes a veto over policies in other areas.

The European Union will have to tackle not only the environment in its own geographical space but also a large part of Central and Eastern Europe. These heavily polluted geographical areas do not have the money to clean up the environment by themselves. They will turn to the European Union. This is where we will see another form of European solidarity arise. If the richer primarily Western and Northern European countries refuse to shoulder that burden, they will lose Central and Eastern Europe. In fact, this question may be one of the most important ones during the negotiations to be held later in the decade concerning the accession of the Central and Eastern European countries to the European Union.

During the 1990s, the richer countries and the Central and Eastern European countries will have to decide how much room the richer countries will allow the poorer countries to maneuver and on what conditions. The problem is that the Central and Eastern European countries do not need to accept the standards of the richer countries in Western and Northern Europe. They can just go on and exercise what later in the decade will be labeled environmental dumping. If they do that, of course, their accession to the European Union will be jeopardized. The implication seems to be that these countries will have to accept certain rules or codes of conduct. If they do, they will get market access and even financial grants to develop their industry.

The European Union itself will, for its members, deal with that question in more or less the same way it dealt with the British nonadherence to the social dimension. If there are some limits to what the nonadhering member state can do and if a certain amount of community regulation is used, it may be accepted. There is an analogy to the articles in the Treaty of Rome concerning state aid. Some kinds of state aid are allowed, and other kinds are allowed under certain conditions; still others are prohibited by the treaty.

The same setup cannot be extended to nonmember states; these states will see much harsher attitudes from the European Union toward the new kinds of international dumping: interest rate policy, social dumping, environmental dumping, and immigration. Countries exercising these types of dumping will find it difficult to get market access unless they enter into specific agreements laying down rules to solve these problems, and it goes without saying that, both parties will find it difficult to conclude such agreements.

Sometime during this decade the European Union will look at two important problems and find that something can be done to solve or at least reduce their significance at the same time: unemployment and the environment.

As it is today, the relative factor prices reflect that labor is scarce and resources are plentiful. That may be right or wrong. The relative prices may be based on the short or long term. The core of the matter is that industrial technology has left us with these relative prices. We act as *homo oeconomicus*, that is, we save labor and we use resources. As a result, we have around 10 percent unemployment, which may be rising, while we deplete the resources to the extent that our generation can be called a generation of resource butchers.

All this simply does not make sense. If we look carefully at the debate, we can see that people are deeply worried about this situation. The remedy is, however, not very difficult to find. Change the relative factor prices. Reduce the price of labor and increase the price of resources. If we do that, we will see the use of labor go up like a rocket while, at the same time, the use of resources will go down.

The tax and subsidy system can be used to accomplish such a change. To be specific, let us take one problem: the milk bottle or rather the nonexisting milk bottle. When I was a boy of ten, the milkman arrived every morning at 5 or 6 o'clock to place the full bottles outside the front door and to pick up the empty bottles. Today we buy paper cartons in the supermarket and throw them away—less use of labor and more use of resources. It is too expensive to deliver and collect bottles while the price of cartons is so low. Change the situation by taxing the use of paper or wood and introduce a more flexible wage system, and we will see the old system reappear.

Thus the tax system will be brought into use during the 1990s to increase—dramatically—the price of resources, and the subsidy system may be brought into play to reduce the price of labor. Many people may not like that because they do not think that such a system is productive. The answer to that is that nonuse of 10 percent of the labor force, while everyone can see where labor could be used, is senseless.

There is, however, one snag: the developing countries. Many of them live by exporting resources. If the richer countries impose a tax that will reduce consumption of resources and cover the economic burden partly to be borne by the developing countries, these countries will have been brought from the ashes into the fire. Therefore, such a policy must be accompanied by a transfer of money from the richer countries to the poorer countries. In fact, we could envisage a system of international assistance where some developing countries are receiving financial assistance according to nonuse of natural resources. The less they use, the more finance is available.

Immigration and asylum are creating problems the European Union would like to ignore, but the union will not be able to escape from them.

It is not very likely that a big influx will come from Central and Eastern Europe and Russia. History tells us that the people who live there are attached to their homelands. The people who have left already were primarily minority groups.

Three groups of immigrants can be envisaged. The first group is made up of refugees from the consequences of war and civil war. If the European Union can prevent such unrest, there will be no war refugees. Economic refugees constitute the second group. If the European Union successfully launches these countries on a reasonable economic growth pattern, the overwhelming part of the populations will stay put. Environmental refugees, the third group, are the most vulnerable and unpredictable ones. One or two major accidents in a nuclear power plant not far from the western border could trigger off a mass of environmental refugees not yet seen in Europe. People know today what such catastrophes may entail for themselves and their families. They will not keep quiet and stay put as they did after the Chernobyl accident in 1986. If the European Union can provide better schemes for environmental protection, such disasters may be preempted.

It will be difficult for the European Union to prepare itself for all these eventualities. It can only be said that a common policy must be established; otherwise, the community solidarity may break. It is not feasible for one or two members of the union to shoulder the overwhelming part of the burden while the rest just rejoice that they were not in the front line.

North Africa is another possible area of immigration into the union. It will be more predictable in the sense that the Southern European countries have for many years taken in large groups of people from the North African states. In view of the fragile political and economic situation there, it cannot be excluded. Suddenly and without much warning, the union may have to face the burden of a large group of refugees from across the Mediterranean.

All experience gained the hard way over centuries and recently along the U.S.–Mexican border shows clearly and unequivocally that it is not possible to close borders completely. Those who have tried have been pushed toward measures that are not compatible with our perception of a democratic society.

Two approaches are necessary. The first one is to map out a common and coherent policy with regard to immigration: which kind of people will we allow into our countries, and which kind of people do we not want. These nasty questions may put us with our backs to the wall, but they cannot be avoided.

The second road consists of a coherent policy to further economic and political development in those countries and areas that host the potential immigrants. Only by convincing the potential immigrants that they can look forward to a decent living in their own countries can we expect them to abandon hopes of emigrating to the European Union. For the union and its citizens, the question is very simple. Do they accept an economic burden in the form of market opening for adjacent poor countries and financial transfers to these countries? If yes, the European Union is willing to share some of its wealth and some of the jobs with adjacent poor countries in the hope that such an approach will keep away any large wave of mass immigration. If no, the implication is that citizens in these countries can obtain a higher living standard only by moving to the European Union to share in the union's the wealth and jobs. It is obvious which approach contains the biggest risk of a social explosion.

Organized Crime

Even if some people do not like to hear it, the open borders following the single market increase the risk of irregular economic activity or outright crime on an international scale. It is a little bit like integration itself—it overtakes the institutional framework. While the answer with regard to integration is a stronger treaty, the answer to organized crime is more cooperation between police forces in member states.

The threats seem to come from various countries. The Sicilian or Italian mafia seems to be expanding in the south of France—or so at least we hear, even if no one really knows. Organized crime is a growing business in the former Soviet Union.

An interesting link exists between crime and immigration in the sense that falsified visas can be bought. So the crime syndicates obtain some of their revenues from people in other states who wish to emigrate to the richer European Union.

Inside the European Union, it can be seen how organized crime moves goods out of the union and into adjacent countries. There can be no doubt that we see organized crime. The police forces can counterattack by a more vigilant attitude and by cooperating with each other. In the medium and longer term, we are back to the same situation we have with immigration and asylum. Only by boosting the economies in adjacent poorer countries can the European Union hope to solve this problem. As it is now, the profit to be gained is so substantial that it is worthwhile to many to run a large risk, which is what these bands do. Only by reducing the potential profit can we hope to eliminate the problem.

In the future, organized crime may adopt even more evil tactics. We all know about blackmail, but we have not yet seen blackmail used to squeeze money out of a national state or government. There is an anxiety about the risk that the Russian mafia has obtained material to produce a nuclear bomb. If so, such a weapon can be used to blackmail governments on a grand scale. In the same mold falls the possibility of the threat of environmental disaster, if demands put by the mafia are not met by the governments. The internationalization combined with the emerging power vacuum in the former Soviet Union paves the way for organized crime on a scale not yet realized.

THE INTERNATIONAL POLICY OF THE EUROPEAN UNION

The European Union cannot follow in the footsteps of the European Community and neglect the outside world and all the problems it brings to the union. The hard fact is that the world is left with one superstate which is questioning its own role. There are increasingly strong signals that the United States is contemplating whether it is still in its interest to be tied up in a multilateral framework constructed after World War II to contain the Soviet Union during the Cold War or whether it should break away from that system. The vital question is whether the United States should remain inside such a multilateral system (amended) or whether the United States should part with more than forty-five years of American policy toward Europe.

The 1990s will not be an easy decade. International competitiveness will be much tougher. That goes for traditional trade policy and for economic and monetary policy as well. The tendency to pass the burden on to other countries or another group of countries will be very strong indeed. Small and medium-sized countries will find it extremely difficult to survive in the new international context unless they are allied with another group of countries.

On top of that, we will see a new kind of international dumping that will pose great problems for the world economy and the world community. We have already discussed the temptation to use the interest rate as a beggar-thy-neighbor instrument to attract the savings surplus from the one area in the world where it will be available, that is, the Far East.

The social dimension introduced by the European Union represents another case in which we will undoubtedly see dumping—social dumping—which the social dimension is designed to prevent. Some member states may wish and actually may try to circumvent the rules, but even so that is insignificant compared to actions by third countries who produce at lower costs based on lower standards for workers. In such a case, the European Union will have to decide whether it will accept the situation or react to it. Acceptance could be accomplished by terms of conditionality attached to development aid. Any reaction will necessitate finding some appropriate rules in international trade policy.

Environmental dumping comes next in line. This question was raised in the Uruguay Round, albeit not in this form. The problem is that some countries, for example, members of the European Union, impose constraints, in the form of rules, taxes, and so on, upon their producers to protect the environment. What happens then when other countries try to export the same kind of products to the union, but cheaper ones because they are not subject to similar rules? How long can the European Union and the United States accept this situation, and what will the developing nations (because we talk about them as exporters) say when the situation is no longer accepted?

Immigration can also be seen in the context of dumping. Some countries are more willing to accept immigrants than others. Accepting immigrants costs money. These more willing countries may conclude that a special kind of social dumping occurs when other countries close their borders which imposes an ever growing burden on them. How long can that situation continue among members of the same group, such as the European Union, or among trading partners?

In short, during the 1990s some very nasty problems may appear under the heading of dumping—problems that will place a considerable strain on the structures governing both our societies and the international community. A solution may require close cooperation among the European Union, the United States, and Japan; otherwise, the system may jam and create social turmoil and economic chaos not unlike what the world saw in the 1930s.

Such a harsh international climate with regard to trade and economic policy may become harsher because the main security link that bound the United States and Europe together during the Cold War has disappeared. In economics and trade the genuine new activity is new kinds of dumping which will force the international community to think differently.

In security policy there is the same need for new thinking. Security policy has for many years been a question of military hardware and the number of soldiers available to protect the borders. That was sensible in an era where the military threat was one of considerable magnitude, which was, indeed, the case with the Soviet armed forces.

Today the situation is completely different. For example, in Denmark, security is not a question of military hardware and the number of soldiers available to defend the borders of Denmark; it is a question of how much Denmark can and will do to stabilize the situation in adjacent countries implementing a reform process under very difficult circumstances. Soldiers and military hardware cannot play a major role in this effort. They may help if they go into peacekeeping forces organized by international institutions and organizations. That military role is, however, entirely different from defending the borders.

The main effort here falls completely outside the sphere of the military forces. It is constituted of economic assistance, trade policies, cultural arrangements, and human factors. It is a question of how much a country can and will do to ensure the smooth implementation of the reform process being undertaken. The notion of security policy for most Western European countries has very little resemblance to our old ideas of security policy. Some countries change track very fast. In 1992 Denmark introduced plans to help countries and regions, mainly in the Baltic, amounting to about 0.25 percent of the gross national product per annum for three years.

The whole philosophy behind this notion of security is that, if we help these countries join the club of democracies with market economies, no military threat will arise in the future. On the other hand, if these countries slide back toward authoritarian regimes, they may rearm and constitute new military threats in the future.

This new concept of security policy is most clearly seen in Northeastern Europe, in the Baltic region. During the last five years, Poland has emancipated itself from the Soviet sphere of influence. The three Baltic States have become sovereign national states. Finland has obtained a new freedom vis-à-vis its big neighbor to the east.

For all these national states, and for their neighbors to the west (Germany, Denmark, Sweden), the notion of security policy has changed completely. Formerly, the national states of Eastern Europe had no security policy problem because they were occupied by Soviet armed forces! For their western neighbors, the problem of security was how to prevent a military attack from the east, and, in case such an attack did materialize, how to defend themselves. This scenario does not make much sense in the political geography of Northeastern Europe in 1994.

The problem now is how to prevent economic and social unrest from occurring in the countries bordering the southeastern coast of the Baltic Sea. If this struggle is lost, all or some of these countries may slide into an abyss with unpredictable but dark futures. They may turn full circle by reentering the arena as authoritarian regimes posing a new military threat to their neighbors. If the struggle is won, however, they may gradually be integrated into a political and economic unity encompassing not only Western Europe but also Central and Eastern Europe.

The question then is how to win the struggle. Military instruments will not be helpful. Economic and financial assistance, market access to Western Europe, and cultural exchanges highlighting the human factor are needed.

In a sense, the new kind of security policy being developed in Europe (a broad security policy encompassing many sectors instead of a narrow security policy based on military instruments alone) may be tested in the Baltic region. Here we have all the ingredients for a new conflict developing into possible military conflicts: small national states surrounded by a large neighbor; ethnic minorities from the large neighbor in the small national states; the small states commanding geographical assets coveted by the larger neighbor; enclaves of one national state between several other national states; historic animosities between the Lithuanians and the Poles, the Russians and the Poles, and the Estonian, Latvian, and Lithuanian distrust of their Russian neighbor. If there is any place where Europe needs a new security policy to help prevent political conflicts it is here.

To understand the development in Europe that has produced this shift of emphasis and change in the notion of security policy, let us start with the role of the United States. The United States has decided to reduce the number of troops in Europe. In the middle of 1994, the number of American troops in Europe was down to approximately 100,000. Europeans will probably have to live with that. The message is quite clear: Europeans cannot count on the Americans to stand guard over European security in the 1990s as they did from 1949 to 1989. The Europeans are on their own in several aspects.

One of these aspects is European security itself. That may not pose any significant problem in the foreseeable future since there is no visible enemy in the area of conventional forces. Europeans should therefore be able to live with that scenario.

Another aspect is that American troops will no longer be present to smooth out any ruffled feathers between the European countries. To put it more bluntly, Europeans will no longer look to the United States to guarantee that Germany will not become too strong. And Germany itself can not any longer hope that an American military presence will alleviate fears about them in other European countries. Time will show whether the Europeans really do trust each other. The risk may be felt most in Eastern Europe, where some countries may not feel comfortable without significant American forces on German soil. Such fears are unwarranted in view of Germany's internal and external policies during the last forty-five years, but they probably still exist.

A third aspect, and the most difficult one, concerns conflicts or wars in adjacent regions or countries. In the former Yugoslavia, Europe has been able to avoid the issue by sidestepping it. The civil wars taking place there have been confined to that area, and no Western European state has intervened to support any one of the warring factions. This posture may not be bad, but it does not solve conflicts. Europe may not have to resort to military force to solve conflicts, but Europe may in the future need to resort to the threat of military force. Otherwise other methods (isolation, sanctions, diplomacy) may not work. To manage a successful foreign and security policy, a nation must be able to fall back on the threat of force as the last resort. In fact, the most successful foreign and security policy threatens the use of military force and, by doing so, creates a margin of maneuver that allows other methods to achieve the objectives.

These three factors mean that, during the 1990s, Europeans will have to make some tough decisions. They may try to skirt the issues, but they will not be able to do so. The actions of the United States may make the decision harder or easier. The more willing the United States seems to be to continue its military presence in Europe, the more likely it is that Europe will choose a path that incorporates a strong link with the United States. The less willing the United States seems to be to maintain a strong military presence, the more likely it is that the Europeans will choose their own way. During the NATO summit held on January 10, 1994, the United States confirmed its commitment to maintain troops in Europe, which alleviated the fears of the Europeans.

For the moment, Europeans are keeping their options open. They have at least three options. One option is to maintain NATO as the mainstay for their defense efforts. That option will mean a strong link with the United States. A second option is to beef up the Western European Union (WEU), which is not incompatible with a continued link with the United States because the WEU is the European pillar in NATO. The former scepticism voiced by the United States with regard to the WEU has been replaced by a positive U.S. stance toward this organization. In this model, the WEU becomes primarily a vehicle for implementing policies in NATO by countries belonging to both organizations. The third option is to build a common defense policy and a common defense system inside the European Union, which would—in theory at least—be the most European option.

Wisely enough, the Europeans are waiting to choose an option until the military threat and the military tasks facing Europe are clearer than they are today. What is sometimes overlooked is that the attitude of the United States may influence the choice. It is not only the potential threat that matters, but also the stance of one's allies. If allies appear to be willing to part ways, this situation must be taken into account when policies are being shaped.

Even if the Treaty on European Union has postponed these questions to 1996, the European Union may not escape all of them in the interval. The developments in the former Yugoslavia have touched a sore spot, and Europeans may not be capable or willing to deal with such issues in adjacent areas. The debate following President Yeltsin's visit to Poland about that country's possibilities for NATO membership is another omen.

Some difficult questions are being asked. Should Europe and the United States put different emphasis on different parts of the former Soviet Union and its former satellites with the unavoidable implication that the United States will give priority to states in possession of nuclear weapons (Russia and Ukraine)? Should NATO be enlarged to include not only Poland but also the Czech Republic, the Slovak Republic, and Hungary; if so, what about Estonia, Latvia, Lithuania, Romania, Bulgaria, and some of the newly born nations in the former Yugoslavia? Has the WEU a role to play and, if so, how will it be defined and, most important, how will it be defined vis-à-vis NATO? Finally, what is the objective of the so-called Balladur initiative, which was floated just after the change of government in Paris in spring 1993? This initiative touches upon several very important issues, among them the question of minorities. There seems to be a niche for the Balladur initiative to deal with some of the unavoidable questions that keep popping up as a consequence of the course toward membership in the European Union for countries in Central and Eastern Europe.

Europeans do not have unlimited time to find the answers to these questions. Such questions do not hide shyly; they may very well ring the doorbell at the moment when they are most unwelcome.

Although Europe's relations to the United States will be dominated by the military vector, its relations to the Far East will be governed by industrial and technological policy combined with economic and monetary policy. Both the European Union and the Far East will have to decide whether they want to cooperate or compete. To a certain extent, this choice may be decided by the role of the United States as a villain or an ally. If the United States decides, during the second half of the 1990s, to become protectionist in economics and trade and isolationist in foreign and security policy, Europe and the Far East may be tempted to join forces to make up for the power vacuum created by the United States.

Neither Europe nor the United States seems to understand the strength and potential of the economic powerhouse building up in the Far East which encompasses from three to five strong growth centers. An omen of what could come in the future was the linkup some years ago between Daimler Benz and Mitsubishi: The Europeans and Japanese discovered that it would be a good idea to do something in common.

An inward-looking United States may push Europe and the Far East into each other's arms. Many of the revolutionary new management policies already take place in European or Japanese enterprises. The linkup between the two old worlds will not occur on a national basis, or state by state, but will take place between enterprises. In fact, the European and Japanese enterprises may jump out of the old mold of national regulations and establish the transnational enterprise as a powerbase that can challenge the sovereignty of the national state (see the last section in chapter 6).

North Africa is a potential trouble spot located not far from the shores of some member states of the European Union. Some of the North African states are highly unstable. The geographical nearness imposes upon the European Union a responsibility not easy to overlook. While Europeans have avoided this issue until now, they may not be able to do so for much longer. Some observers regard these countries as potential powder kegs. Sometime during the 1990s North Africa may force Europeans to make some unpleasant decisions.

At the end of the decade, the European Union will have two major adjacent foreign problems: Russia and Turkey. Turkey applied for membership in the 1980s in accordance with the association agreement. The community has managed to keep Turkey waiting, but there is a time limit. Turkey, a growing economic and political power, occupies a strategic position. Sooner or later Turkey will demand a clear answer, and, as time goes by, it may be sooner rather than later. The European Union will be forced to make a genuine foreign policy decision. Is it preferable to keep Turkey outside as a buffer state to the Middle East, or should Turkey be included in the European Union? The answer given by the European Union and the way it is delivered will govern relations between Turkey and the European Union for centuries. It should not be overlooked that, for several centuries, a large part of European history consisted of competition and even armed struggle between Europe and Turkey. The notion of the Ottoman empire was almost completely absent from the vocabulary of modern Turkey until a few years ago. Now it seems that a cultural, economic, and perhaps even political expansion into the Islamic parts of the former Soviet Union is entering the minds of many Turks. Furthermore, Turkey has become an important investor in many countries adjacent to it.

Russia presents just as difficult a problem. Few would dispute that Russia cannot become a member of the European Union. Having said that, most observers would add that neither can Russia manage without some kind of close association to the European Union. Europe does not end at the former borders between the Hapsburg and Romanov empires. It goes on at least to the Urals and possibly still further. While the European Union may stop at some point, in Eastern Europe the notion and idea of Europe do not.

There is no straightforward solution. Russia is not only a large country, but a great nation with proud traditions. It welcomes without any doubt assistance from Europe, but not in any way that indicates some kind of submission. Assistance must be granted a platform that signals that Europe and Russia are on an equal footing. If the European Community does not appraise correctly the long-term consequences of an unfortunate attitude to Russia, they may make a terrible mistake. Russia and the Russians are down on their knees for the moment, but sooner or later they will claim their rightful position among nations. At that time, it would be best if Russia and the European Community could launch a partnership without reproaching each other for anything that happened in the past.

Some Europeans no doubt will be tempted to emulate the American attitude toward Europe in the immediate postwar period. That patron-client, or center-hinterland, relation worked for a time, but it will not work any longer. Europe is no longer comfortable in the role of client or hinterland to the United States. Europe should learn from that experience when shaping its foreign and security policy toward its adjacent areas, primarily Russia and Turkey, but also North Africa and probably the Middle East.

Europe should also realize that there is a fundamental difference between what Europe is today and what the United States was forty-five years ago. The United States could, if the need arose, lean back on a military arsenal more powerful than anything else in the world. Europe cannot do so. As history tells us, the United States has from time to time actually used this military arsenal. *Ultima Ratio Regum* was not an empty phrase. Europe will have to steer its course in waters just as troublesome but without this fallback position. It can be done only by rapidly building up a much broader and more sophisticated foreign and security policy. Success will entail the skillful use of old historical ties and genuine understanding of centuries of lessons in good and bad behavior.

Finally, sooner or later, Europeans need to find out how much or how little they want to be able to point to the phrase *Ultima Ratio Regum* even if they do not want to apply military means to achieve political objectives.

A new major war in the European theater is not unthinkable but it is unlikely. What is less unlikely is the occurrence of a whole string of ethnic conflicts in Europe. If we base ourselves on the analysis put forward in this book, it is not difficult to see where these conflicts might take place: in a band about 1,000 kilometers wide from Finland in the north to Greece in the south. This is where culture and political borders for nearly a thousand years meet, indeed clash! West of this band, the Catholic Church and Protestantism are the basic cultures. The Hapsburg empire and the German-inspired states as political entities rarely reached beyond this band. East of the band are the Orthodox Church and Islam. As political entities, we have the empire of the Russian czars (replaced by the Soviet empire) and the Ottoman empire.

The interesting thing in Europe is not these three empires vis-à-vis each other but the geographical areas where they clash: in Central and Eastern Europe. The classic example is the former Yugoslavia where we have Slovenia and Croatia in the Catholic camp and Serbia in the Orthodox camp (for a time conquered by Islam). In between, we have Bosnia-Herzegovina, a cultural buffer state in Europe for more than 1,500 years. In fact, the most likely spot in all Europe for an ethnic, religious, and linguistic conflict (a conflict about culture) is Bosnia-Herzegovina. No wonder it came.

Future conflicts in Europe can be classified according to the following criteria: ethnic conflicts, ecological conflicts, the issue of refugees, and economic and social conditions.

Ethnic conflicts pose the strongest danger toward the future of Europe. Such conflicts loom in Central and Eastern Europe, but they are not totally out of the question in certain areas of Western Europe. We would be wise, however, to concentrate our attention on the band running from north to south in Central and Eastern Europe.

Ecological conflicts present a new type of conflict unforeseen and disregarded, very unwisely, by traditional political scientists. The conflict between Slovakia and Hungary over the dam stemming the Donau near Bratislava is an example. We should not overlook that big differences in environmental protection in different parts of Europe constitute a potential source of conflict. The safety of nuclear power stations in the former Soviet Union is another case in point. Furthermore, the Central and Eastern European countries are not capable of making payments in case of such disasters, and some of the damage will be felt in Western Europe. Paying for actual damage may be easier than sharing the costs to prevent such disasters. Adjacent countries may ask for precautionary measures that the home country is not willing to pay for.

A strong influx of refugees from an adjacent national state may impose such a burden that conflict could develop. This may be both a political and economical problem. Who is going to pay? If the home country actually encourages people to leave or does not do anything to prevent it, the costs may not be sustainable for the receiving country. This problem was foreseen during the negotiations on the Maastricht Treaty, and some of these problems were negotiated during the intergovernmental conference.

Economic and social conditions pose a fourth source of conflict. Europe is in a race to help the Central and Eastern European countries succeed in developing satisfactory economic and social conditions making it worthwhile for their populations to stay at home instead of contemplating mass immigration into Western Europe. That race may determine Europe's future for many years into the next century.

For Europeans, these themes constitute another and totally different threat than the one they got accustomed to during the Cold War. They cannot count on the United States to solve these problems as they could when they faced the heavily armed bear. They have not developed sufficiently effective instruments in what we may call the soft area of security policy (economics, finance, trade, culture, human relations) to take over from the hard option (military instruments). They have not built the necessary organizations to cope with all these challenges. The Europeans, however, are on their way. They do more or less the right things. The question is whether they will do enough and whether they will be able to adjust in the time span available.

Peace and stability demand an approach based upon the following guidelines.

1. The soft options of security policy must be given higher priority. Economic measures, financial assistance, trade, culture, and human relations must be upgraded substantially. They need to be given a higher priority even if that means less funding for the military sector. The threshold for use of military force is higher for Europeans than it has been for Americans in other parts of the world. One reason is that Europe will apply security policy in adjacent countries.

2. It is, however, a mistake to believe that we can do away with the military sector. The soft options of security policy can work effectively only if the powers in question can resort to credible military forces. It must be understood that force will be used if and when a situation demanding the use of force arises. This last point is more important than many people realize.

The military vector must be based upon two fundamental almost eternal guidelines for security and defence policies. The first one says that security cannot be divided. You cannot work in any geographic area with or without some allies. When you have chosen your allies you must stick with them. Any attempt to flirt with other allies entails a deadly risk toward your vital alliance. The second one says that any security guarantee needs to be credible to deter a potential enemy. Otherwise it will not work. Worse than that, it may even call the whole construction into question in the sense that the enemy thinks he can call your bluff and by doing so weaken you mortally. The British and French guarantee to

Poland before the outbreak of World War II in 1939 is a precise example of this. Everybody knew that the British and the French could not defend Poland. Sometimes somebody can be tempted by handing out security guarantees, but it will always be a wise course to analyze whether it is credible and can be honored.

3. The European Union must move its frontiers forward to encompass a large number of the Central and Eastern European countries. It must happen now when it is not regarded as an affront by Russia. The conflicting messages from Russia with regard to NATO membership for Poland—and by implication for the Visegrad countries—clearly indicate how difficult it will be to stage such a maneuver if Russia adopts a sullen attitude, or worse a negative position. Europe must move ahead in such a manner that it is the European Union and not some small or medium-sized Eastern European countries nor Germany which Russia—in much better shape from ten to twenty years from now—will encounter in the central and eastern part of Europe.

The objective is not to make another military alliance directed against Russia in the same way NATO was a military alliance directed against the Soviet Union. That would be the easiest thing to do. The objective is to provide the Central and Eastern European countries with a security guarantee without alienating Russia from the European concert. This is complicated but imperative.

4. The different European organizations must be used fully. The centerpiece to ensure peace and stability is the European Union. In fact, two enlargements of the union are at hand: the EFTA countries and the Central and Eastern European countries. The French initiative, in the form of the Balladur pact, has a very important role to play as a road map toward full membership for the Central and Eastern European countries.

Membership in the WEU of a whole string of small and medium-sized European countries may be less provocative to Russia than membership in NATO. Even if the NATO members do not recognize a Russian say in these things, it is wise not to act in any way that makes the Russians feel that their security is being threatened. If that happens, Europeans would just have swapped insecurity among the members of the European family instead of increasing security in the whole of Europe. Here, as is the case for economic integration, only if all states involved benefit can the enterprise be classified a success. That is what is called "the positive sum game."

In May 1994 the WEU decided to offer associate partnership to nine Central and Eastern European countries. The main idea is that the course of these countries toward membership in the European Union should be accompanied by a similar movement toward the Western European Union. This underlines the WEU as some kind of bridge between the European Union and NATO. The American scepticism toward the WEU, replaced during the second half of 1993 and beginning of 1994 by benevolence, reflects the American wish that the Europeans shoulder more of the burden for the defense of Western Europe themselves. The United States therefore welcomes WEU as the European pillar in NATO.

NATO should gradually and carefully feel its way forward, not only for future membership but also for future strategy. The situation today is more complicated than it was during the last forty years when NATO was the only organization capable of guaranteeing security. NATO is still the most powerful, indeed the only, organization capable of delivering when it really counts. The main new thing in Europe is that the probability for such an occasion to arise has decreased steeply during the last three to five years. The traditional NATO (vintage 1949) is less well equipped to tackle the type of conflict that is now more likely to occur, and it is not well equipped to enter into the business of preventive diplomacy which, by all accounts, will be the centerpiece of security policy in Europe.

The introduction of Partnership for Peace (PFP), agreed upon at the summit held on January 10, 1994, aims exactly at remedying this situation. It offers to a whole range of countries not belonging to the circle of NATO members a closer relation to the alliance. Although it is not membership, it goes some way toward membership, and it keeps open the prospect of membership at a later date. It has been welcomed by the Central and Eastern European countries. In a way it can be called preventive diplomacy by a military alliance—an interesting new concept.

The future of NATO will be determined not only by European but also by American behavior and perception of the future. The problem is to redefine the role of this organization and to do it in a way that maintains an American military presence in Europe without alienating the Russians.

This is where the stakes are highest. For all other initiatives, Europeans may map out where to go and how to get there. A mistake or a wrong judgment with regard to the future of NATO will not be easy to remedy.

Some people take the view that the CSCE as a loose organization may lose weight in the years ahead. That may well be so, but we should not overlook that the CSCE offers some indispensable tools to Europeans. It has played a useful role hitherto and will undoubtedly continue to do so. It may not be the most glamorous organization but, that does not make it superfluous.

Most people see the enlargement of the European Union in the context of an economic and technological enterprise. This is true, but only to a certain extent. The underlying power behind the enlargement is security policy.

Sweden, heavily industrialized, wants to join the European Union to boost its economy. Finland, as a neighbor to Russia, looks at membership in the European Union as a safeguard just in case the northeastern part of Europe turns nasty again. Norway, a NATO member, is adjacent to the large Russian base at Murmansk in the Kola Peninsula. The counterweight to the heavy Russian military arsenal is the United States through NATO, but there is no guarantee that this will last forever. If the United States disengages itself from the Western European theater, the climate could grow uncomfortable for Norway without some link to a possible European defense identity. Austria, in the middle of Europe, is not in the firing line of any foreseeable military conflict.

Future membership in the European Union for the Central and Eastern European countries, including the Baltic States, is linked to the enlargement with the EFTA countries inasmuch as this enlargement must be accomplished before negotiations can start with the Central and Eastern European countries, who regard membership primarily as a matter of security. They want some kind of guarantee in case the world changes back to the bad old days. The problem is how to provide such a guarantee at a time in history when Europe does not possess a defense policy of its own, when Russia is sensible with regard to its own status, and when the future military presence in Europe of the United States is not as certain as it once was.

The answer is to provide an implicit security guarantee through the prospect of membership in the European Union. As long as that is credible, the said countries will feel reasonably secure, and Russia will rest assured that the guarantee is not pointed directly at a possible Russian military aggression. All parties are content with the tacit understanding that military aggression or threats against a future member of the European Union is unlikely.

If the enlargement of the European Union with the EFTA countries fails, the Central and Eastern European countries would lose the prospect of this implicit guarantee. How would they react to that? Probably by asking for a much more direct security guarantee from the Western powers and probably by executing that wish by asking for membership in NATO. They would feel that the prospect of being in where it really matters—the European Union—had faded, and in these circumstances there would be no real alternative to seeking membership in NATO. That would land another problem on the table for Western Europe and the United States. Russia would find itself in an uncomfortable situation and without much doubt would react in a way so as not to be misunderstood.

The enlargement of the European Union with first the EFTA countries and then the Central and Eastern European countries, including the Baltic States, is the vehicle for solving the problem of European security in a way that will be acceptable to all parties and countries concerned. If it goes wrong, Europe will, in a very short time, be faced with a string of awkward and sensitive decisions with regard to security policy and security guarantees.

NOTE

1. Report on the role of public finances in European integration published by the EEC Commission, Brussels, April 1977.

8

Conclusion

All indications are that the European Union and Europe itself are approaching the stage where major decisions will be made to map out the future European model. History tells us that the following factors are instrumental in signaling that the embryonic stage is being replaced by a more mature age:

1. The appearance of institutions worth of that name in the sense that they are capable of sustaining a political process. The European Union may not yet qualify as such an institution. Not many would agree that the European institutions have found their final stage, but the skeleton of an institutional structure can be seen.

2. Money—in two respects: powers to tax and to spend. To a certain extent and inside a limited amount, the European Union does have these powers. A common currency is planned but has not yet been implemented.

3. Soldiers—the ability to defend national interests, if the need arises, with military power. That is not yet the case, but the treaty includes provisions pointing toward such a possibility.

4. Symbols. The European Union possesses an anthem, a flag, and so on, which transmit clear signals to citizens.

The stage is thus set for a decade full of excitement and far-reaching decisions. All the ingredients are in place. This is occurring when Europe must shape its future under the influence of several significant, new orientations.

1. The transition from the industrial to the immaterial society.

2. The replacement of a world order with the United States as the indisputable leader possessing military, economic, and cultural supremacy by a more complicated world order; at first, tripolar but gradually settling into a power game dominated by transnational economic centers and supranational enterprises.

3. A stronger economic integration and a more international world.

4. A stronger drive for cultural decentralization by individual peoples wishing to shape their own cultures and their own identities while the hitherto dominant Anglo-Saxon culture is under attack.

During the 1990s, Europe must meet the following challenges:

1. A double economic challenge: in the high-technology sector from the United States and Japan; in the low-technology, labor-intensive, and low-price sectors from developing countries and some parts of Central and Eastern Europe.

2. The large number of European countries wanting to join the European Union. For some, that poses political problems; for others, it poses economic problems. For a few, it seems to be a smooth process.

3. The risk of conflicts in geographical Europe like the one we have seen in the former Yugoslavia.

4. Immigration from adjacent, less affluent countries.

5. Improving the environmental standard in the European Union itself, contributing to the cleanup of Central and Eastern Europe and the former Soviet Union, and at the same time coping with the problem of the lower environmental standards of many trading partners.

Select Bibliography

Albert, Michel, and James Ball. *Towards European Economic Recovery in the 1980s*. Report to the European Parliament. New York: Praeger, 1984.

Armstrong, John Alexander. *Nations before Nationalism*. Chapel Hill: University of North Carolina Press, 1982.

Aron, Raymond. *Peace and War: A Theory of International Relations*. 1966. Reprint. New York: Anchor Press, 1973.

———. *Main Currents in Sociological Thoughts*. Vol. 2. 1967. Reprint. Durkheim, Pareto, Weber, London: Penguin, 1970.

Attali, Jacques. *Lignes d'Horizons*. Paris: Fayard, 1990.

———. *Europe(s)*. Paris: Fayard, 1994.

Bell, Daniel. *The Cultural Contradictions of Capitalism*. New York: Basic Books, 1976.

Bloom, William. *Personal Identity, National Identity and International Relations*. Cambridge, England: Cambridge University Press, 1990.

Buchan, David. *Europe—The Strange Superpower*. Aldershot: Dartmouth Publishing Company, 1993.

Carlson, Richard, and Bruce Goldman. *2020 Visions*. Stanford, Calif.: Stanford University Press, 1990.

———. *FAST FORWARD: Where Technology, Demographics, and History Will Take America and the World in the Next Thirty Years*. New York: HarperBusiness, 1994.

Carrère d'Encausse, Hélène. *L'Empire éclaté. La Revolte des nations en URSS*. Paris: Flammarion, 1978.
————. *La Gloire des nations ou la fin de l'Empire soviétique*. Paris: Fayard, 1990.
Commission of the European Communities. *Report on Economic and Monetary Union in the European Community*. Luxembourg, 1989.
————. *Policies on Immigration and the Social Integration of Migrants in the European Community*. Sec. (90) 1813. Brussels: September 28, 1990.
————. *Growth, Competitiveness, Employment*. Commission white paper. Luxembourg, 1993.
Garten, Jeffrey E. *A Cold Peace: America, Japan, Germany, and the Struggle for Supremacy*. 1992.
Hobsbawm, E. J. *Nations and Nationalism since 1870: Programme, Myth, Reality*. Cambridge, England: Cambridge University Press, 1990.
Kissinger, Henry. *Diplomacy*. New York: Simon and Shuster, 1994.
Michaelski, Anna, and Helen Wallace. *The European Community: The Challenge of Enlargement*. London: Riia, 1992.
Møller, J. Ørstrøm. *Technology and Culture in a European Context*. København: Handelshøjskolens Forlag, 1991.
Pool, Ethiel de Sola. *Technologies of Freedom*. Cambridge, Mass.: Harvard University Press, 1983.
Putti, Joseph. *Management Asian Context*. Singapore: McGraw-Hill, 1990.
Putti, Joseph, and Audrey Chia. *Culture and Management*. Singapore: McGraw-Hill, 1991.
Schmidheiny, Stephan. *Changing Course*. Cambridge, Mass.: MIT Press, 1992.
Sellier, André, and Jean Sellier. *Atlas des Peuples d'Europe Centrale*. La Découverte, 1992.
Story, Jonathan, ed. *The New Europe*. Oxford: Blackwell, 1993.
Taylor, A.J.P. *The Habsburg Monarchy*. London: Penguin, 1948.
Thurow, Lester. *Head to Head*. New York: Morrow, 1992.
Todd, Emmanuel. *L'Invention de l'Europe*. Paris: Seuil, 1990.
Toffler, Alvin and Heidi. *War and Anti-War*. New York: Little Brown and Company, 1993.
Wæver, Ole. "Conflicts of Vision: Vision of Conflict." In *Identity, Migration and the New Security Agenda in Europe*, edited by Ole Wæver, Barry Buzan, Morten Kelstrup, and Pierre Lemaitre, 283–325. London: Pinter, 1989.
————. *Hele Europa: Projekter, Kontraster*. Copenhagen: SNU, 1989.
————. "Three Competing Europes: German, French, Russion." *International Affairs* 66, 3 (1990): 477–99.
Wæwer, Ole, Barry Buzan, Morten Kelstrup, and Pierre Lemaitre. *Identity, Migration and the New Security Agenda in Europe*. London: Pinter, 1993.

Wallace, William. *The Transformation of Western Europe*. London: RIIA/ Pinter, 1990.

———. *The Dynamics of European Integration*. London: RIIA/Pinter, 1990.

———. "Sovereignty: As a Political Concept in Its Historical Setting." Paper presented at the annual conference of the British International Studies Association, Newcastle, England, December 1990.

Wilson, Edward O. *Sociobiology: The New Synthesis*. Cambridge, Mass.: Harvard University Press, 1975.

Yergin, Daniel, and Thane Gustafson, *Russia 2010*. New York: Random House, 1993.

Index

About the Author

J. ØRSTRØM MØLLER is State Secretary in the Danish Ministry of Foreign Affairs. He is a noted commentator on European affairs and one of
the most influential negotiators in the European Community, particularly
in the areas of trade and economic affairs. Mr. Møller is the author of
over twenty books published in Europe and holds a Cand. Polit. from
the University of Copenhagen.

ISBN 0-275-95012-3

90000>

EAN

9 780275 950125

HARDCOVER BAR CODE